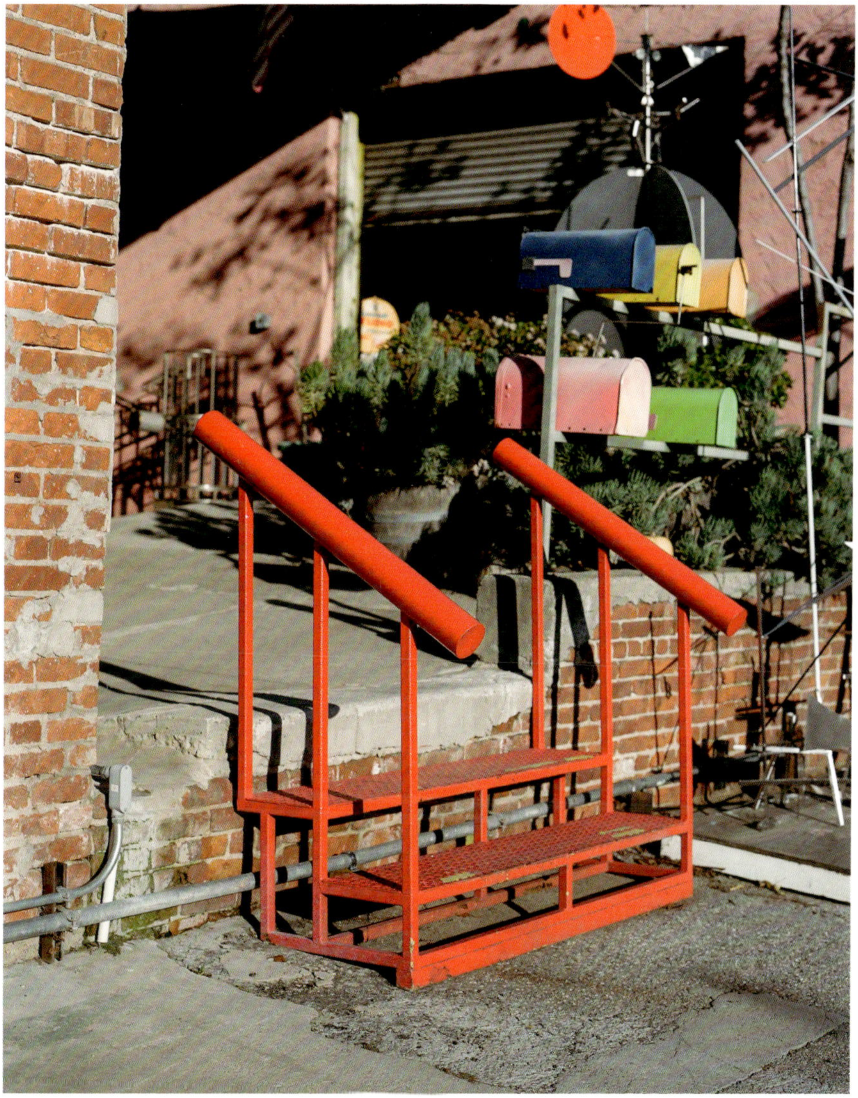

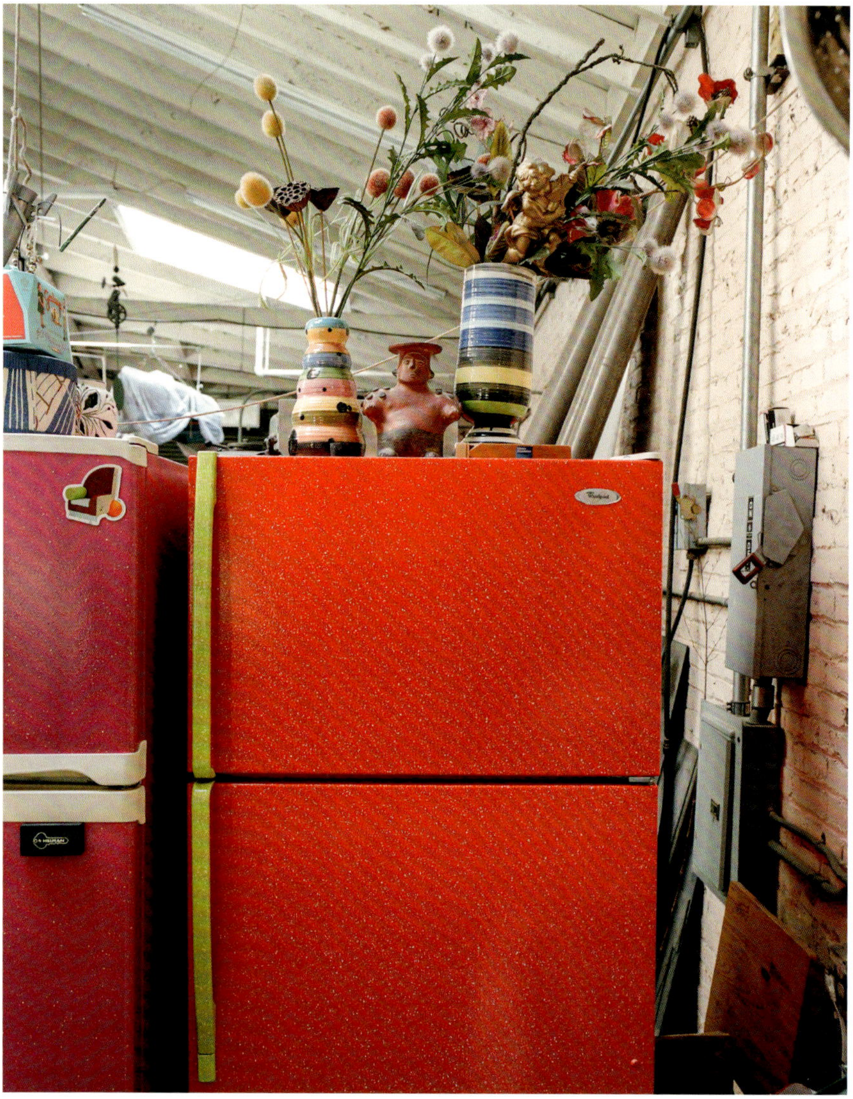

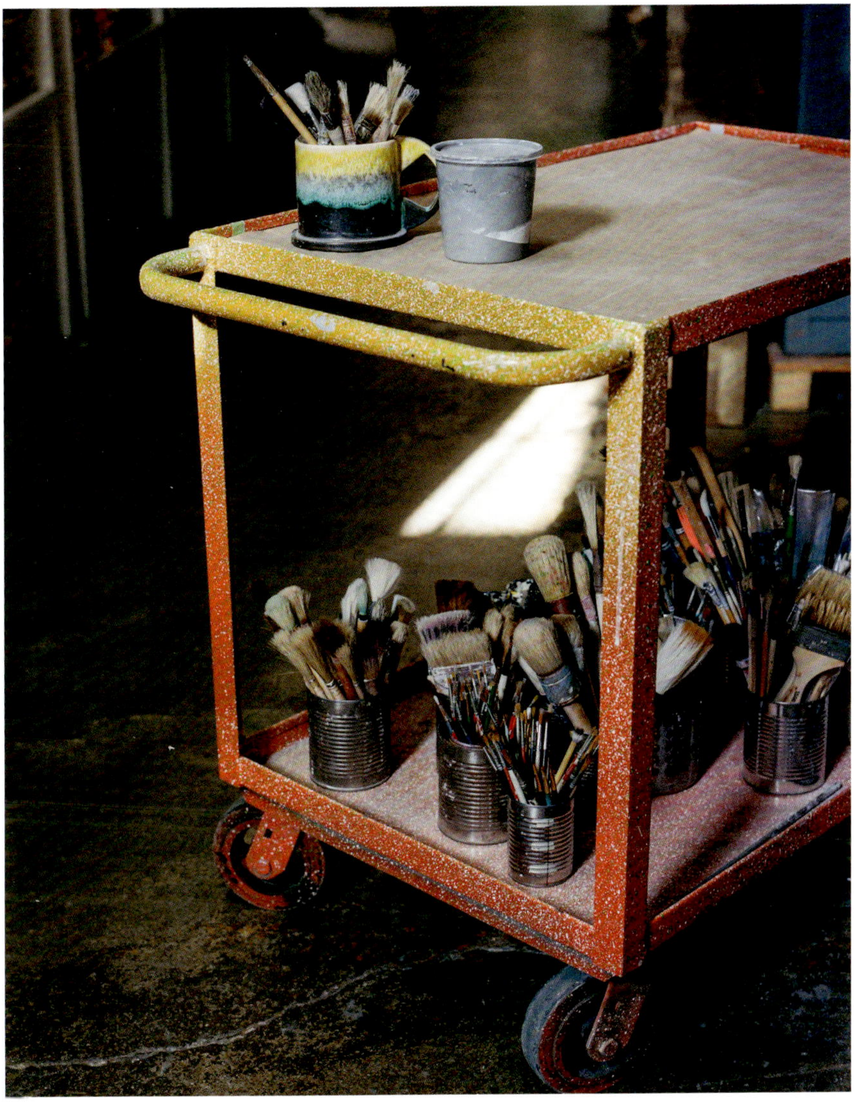

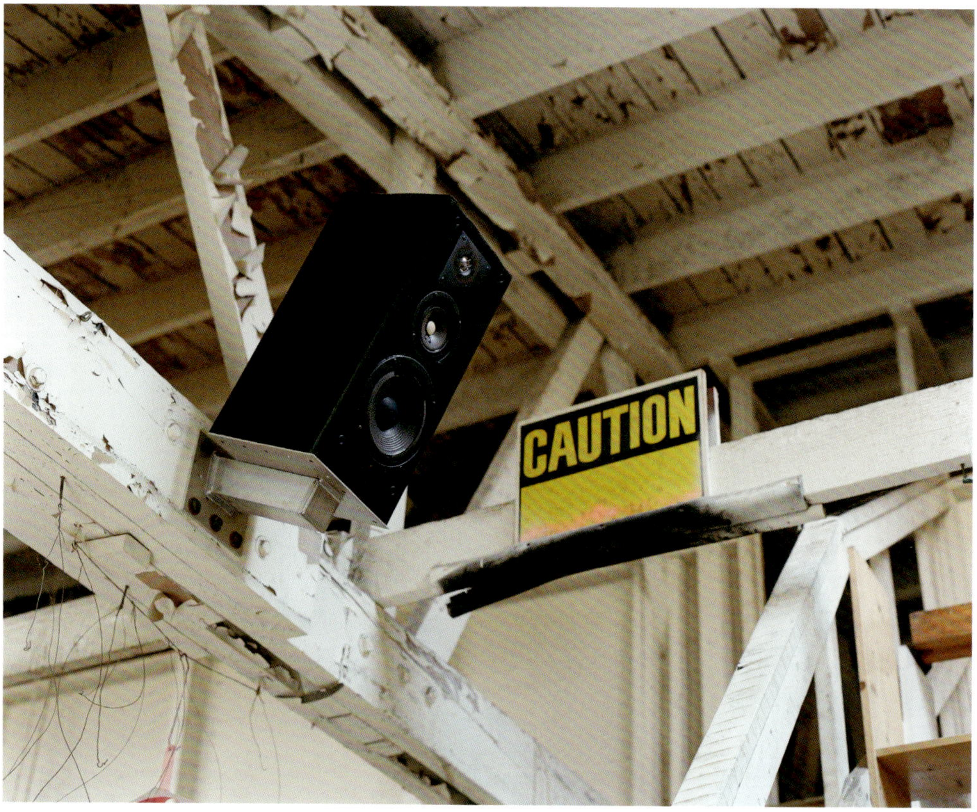
CAUTION

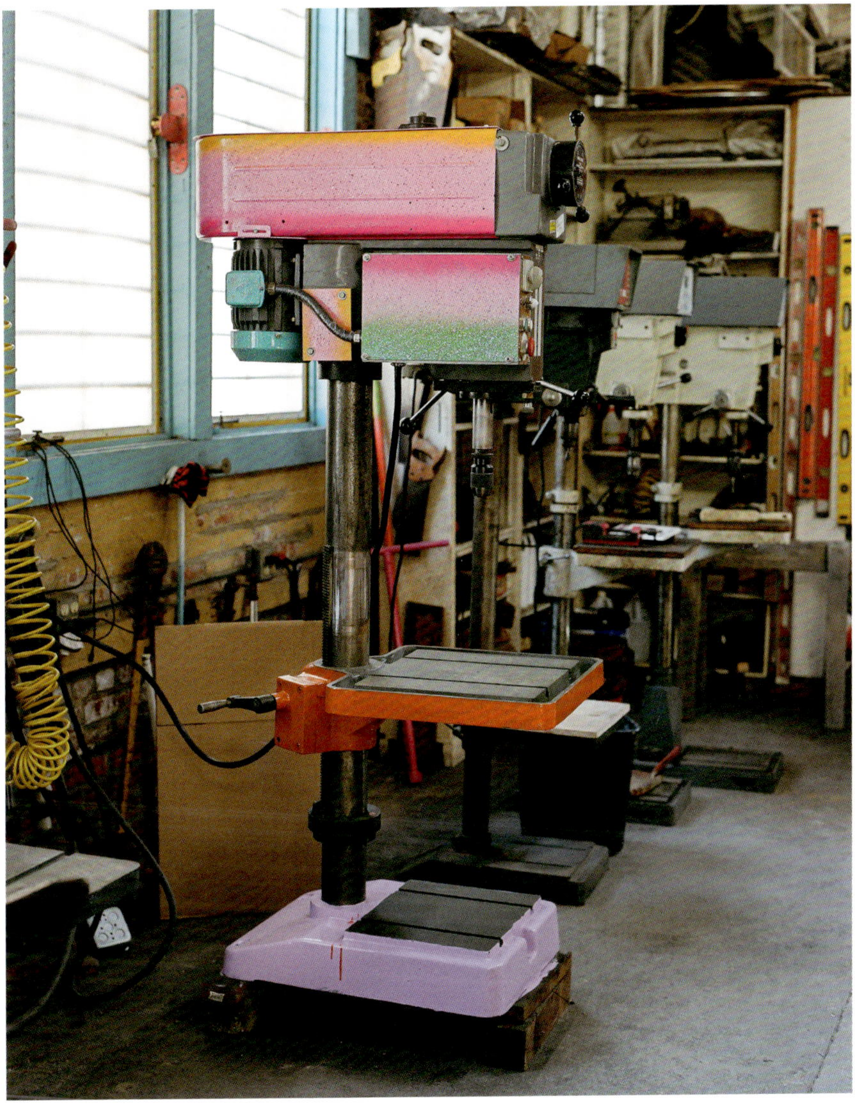

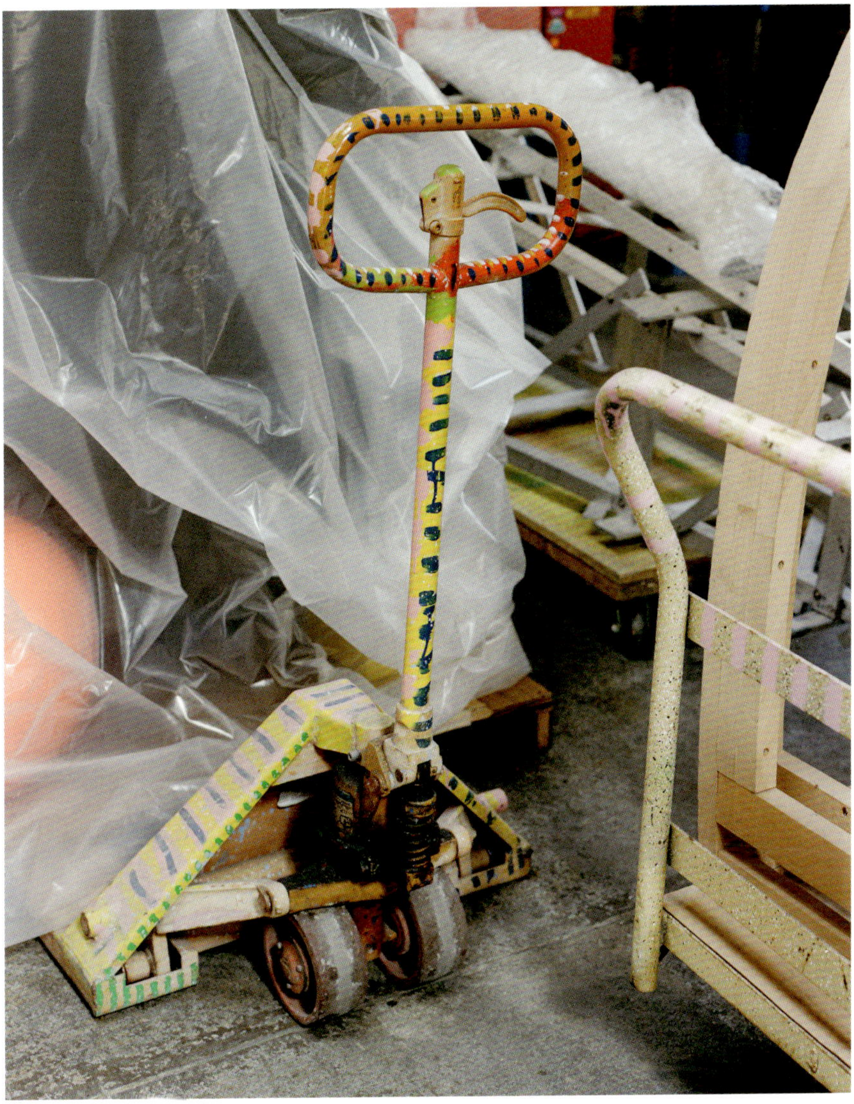

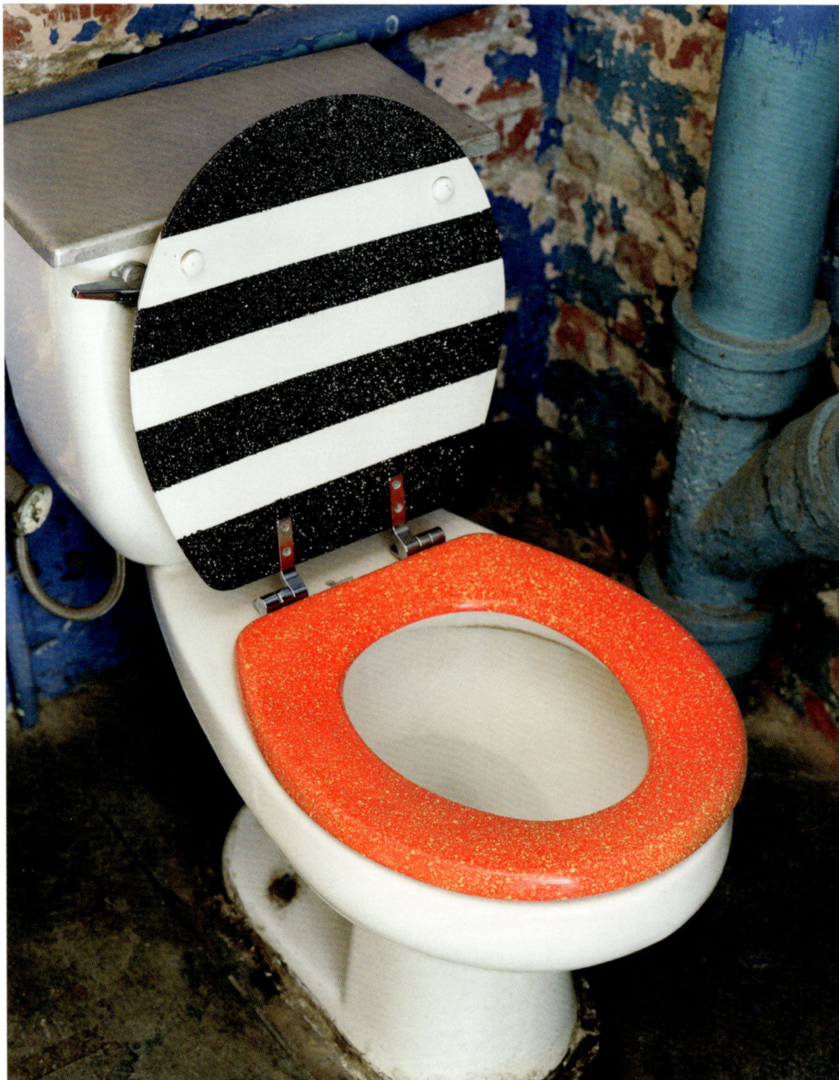

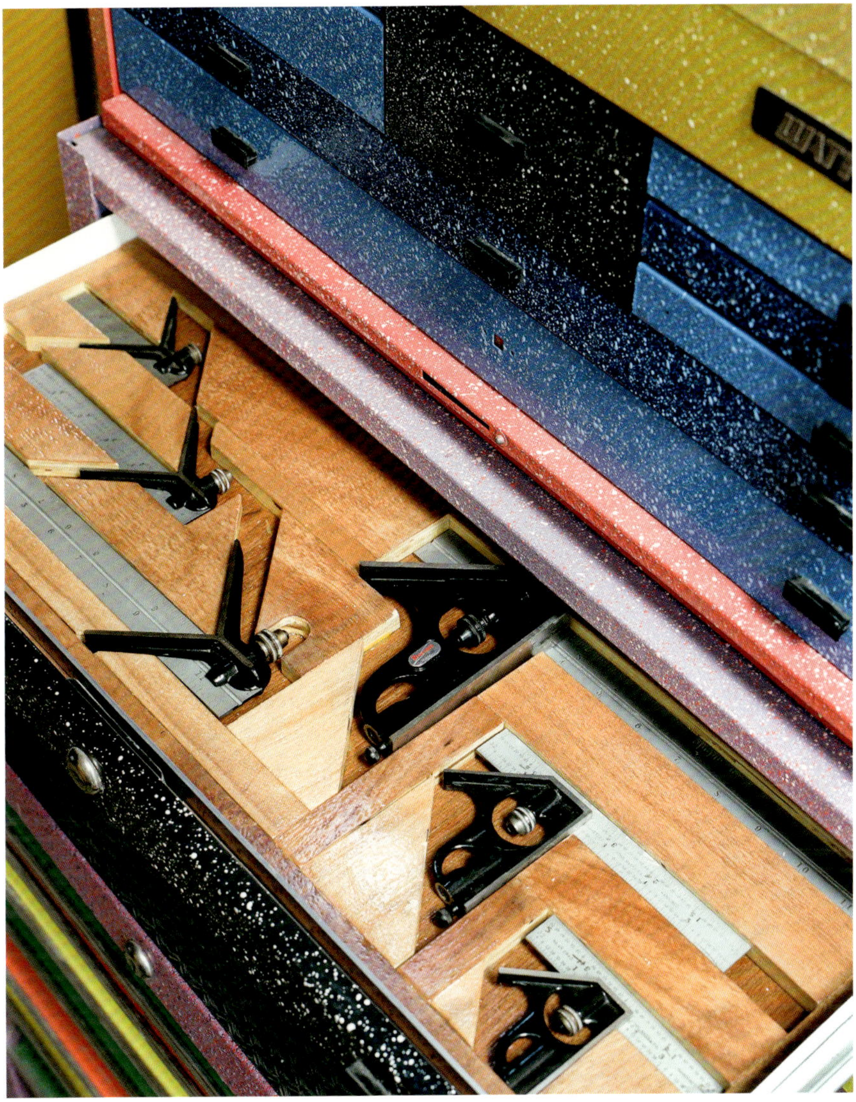

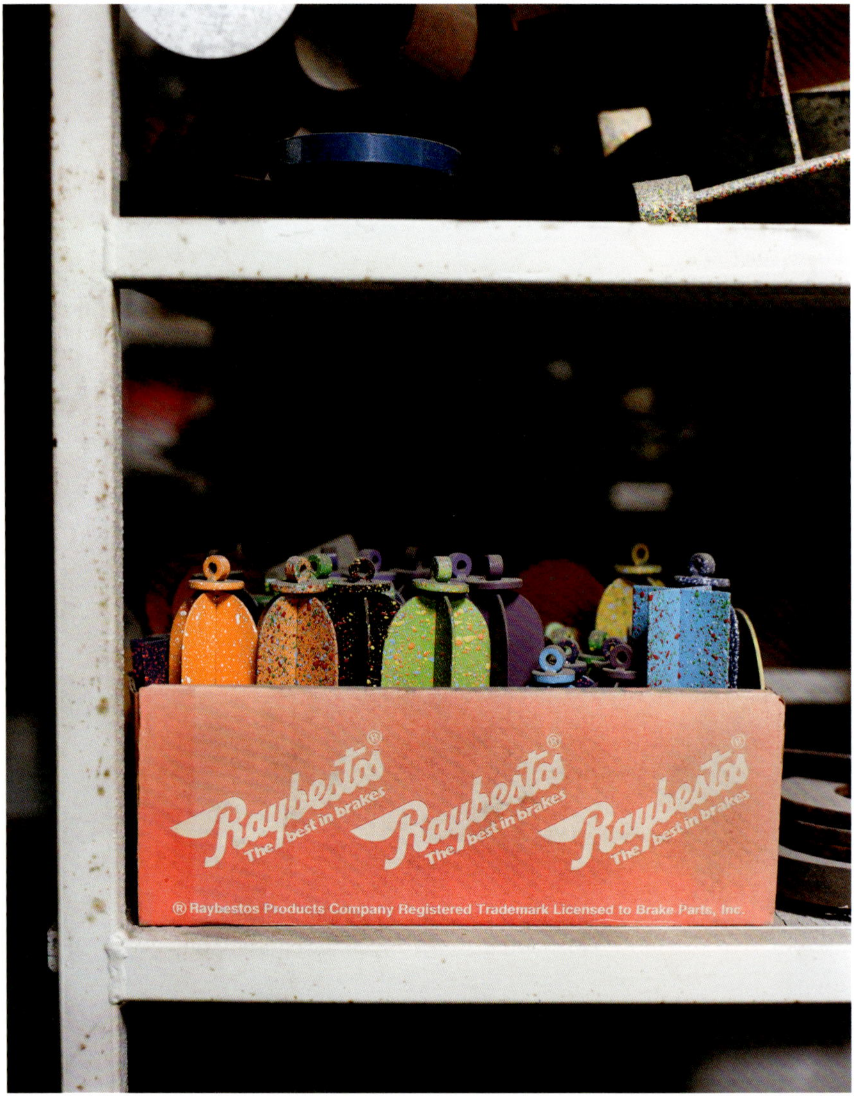
Raybestos® The best in brakes
Raybestos® The best in brakes
Raybestos® The best in brakes
® Raybestos Products Company Registered Trademark Licensed to Brake Parts, Inc.

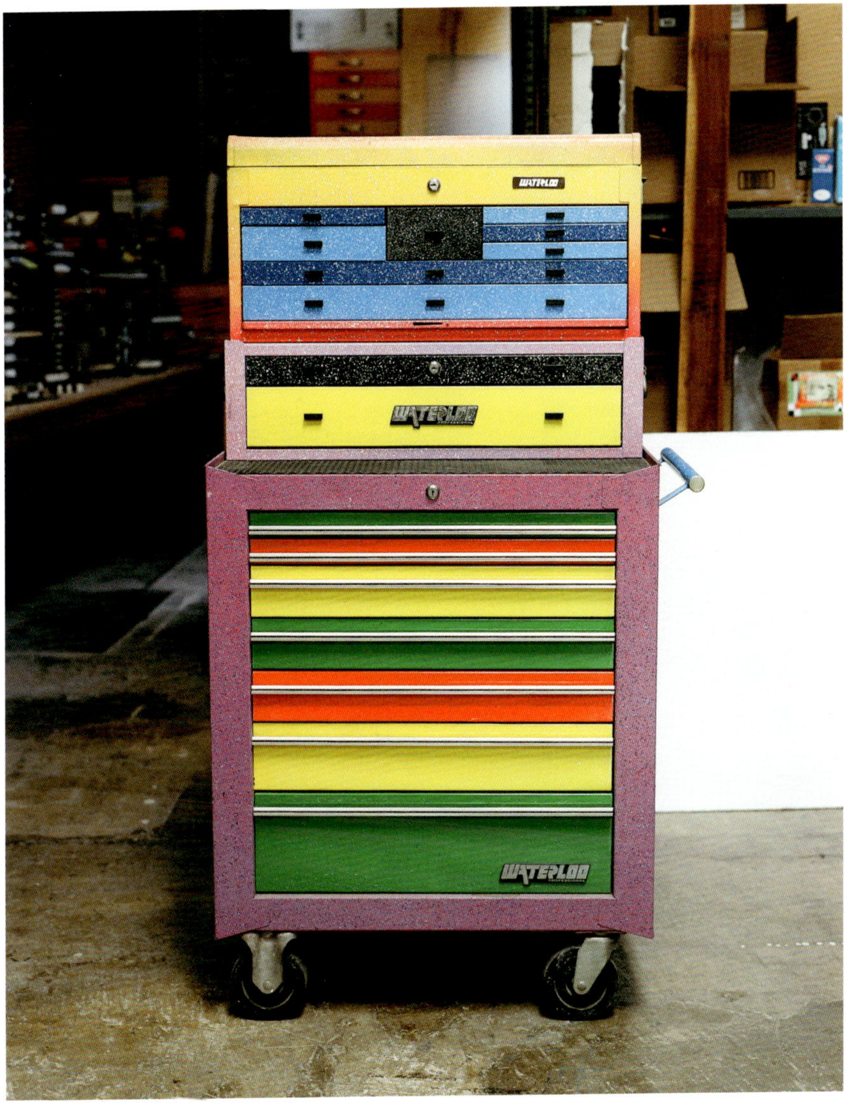
WATERLOO
WATERLOO
WATERLOO

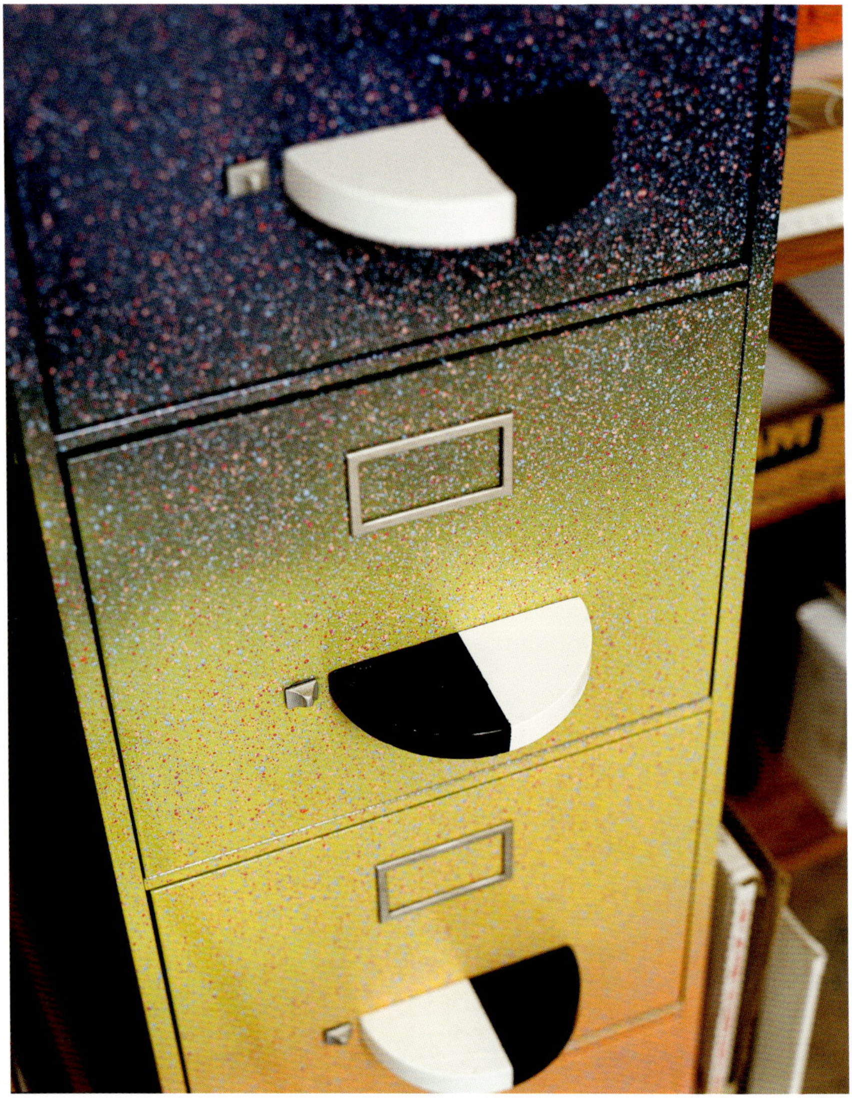

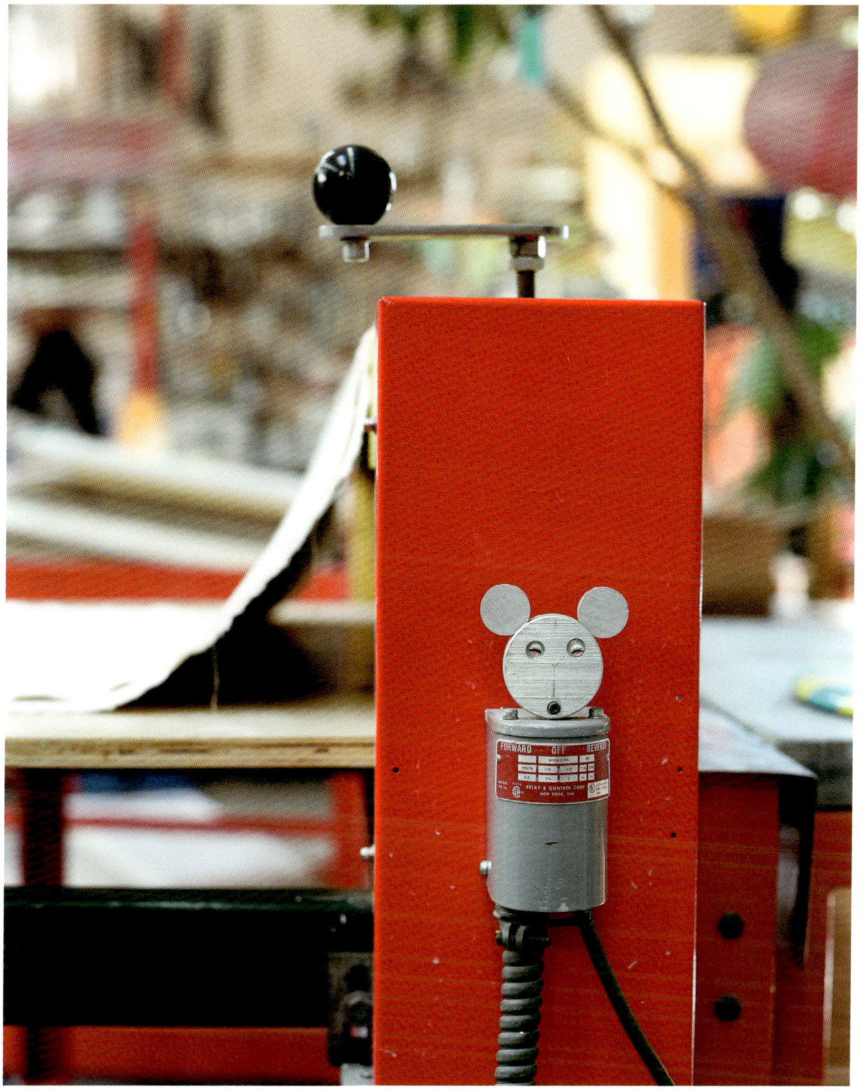
FORWARD
OFF
RELAY & CONTROL CORP.
NEW YORK, USA

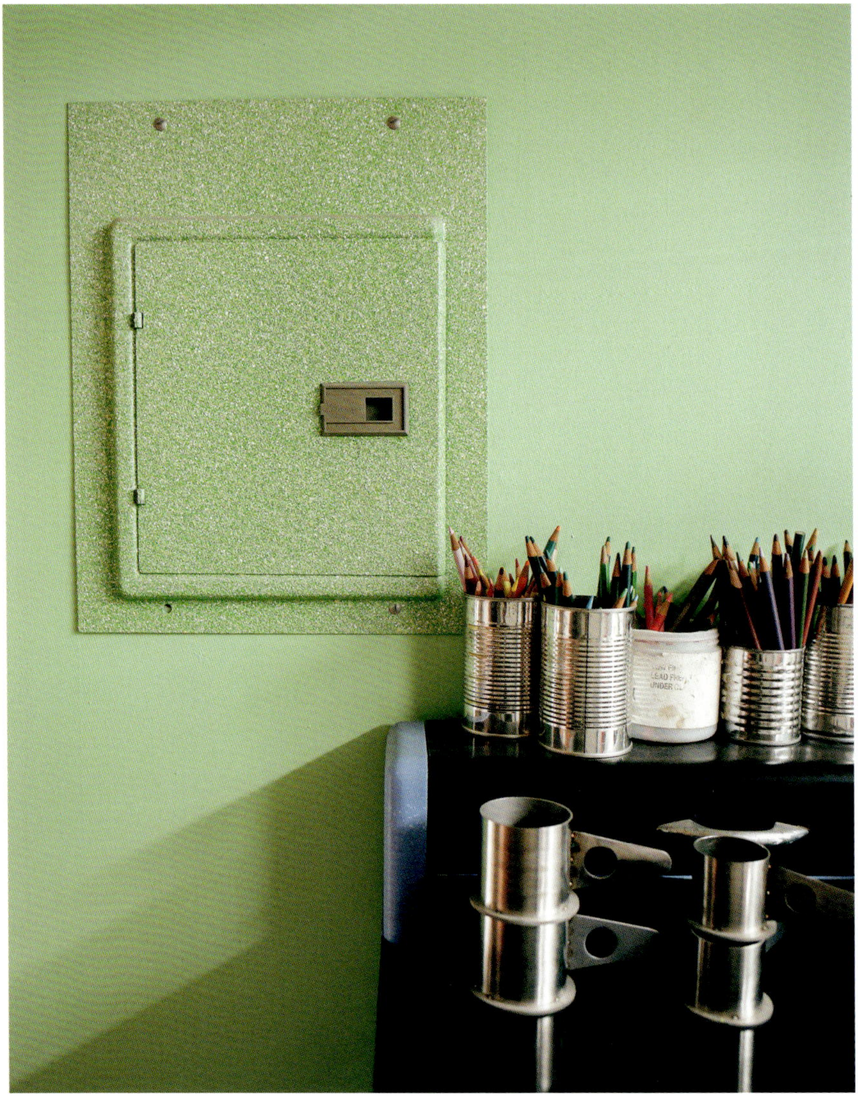

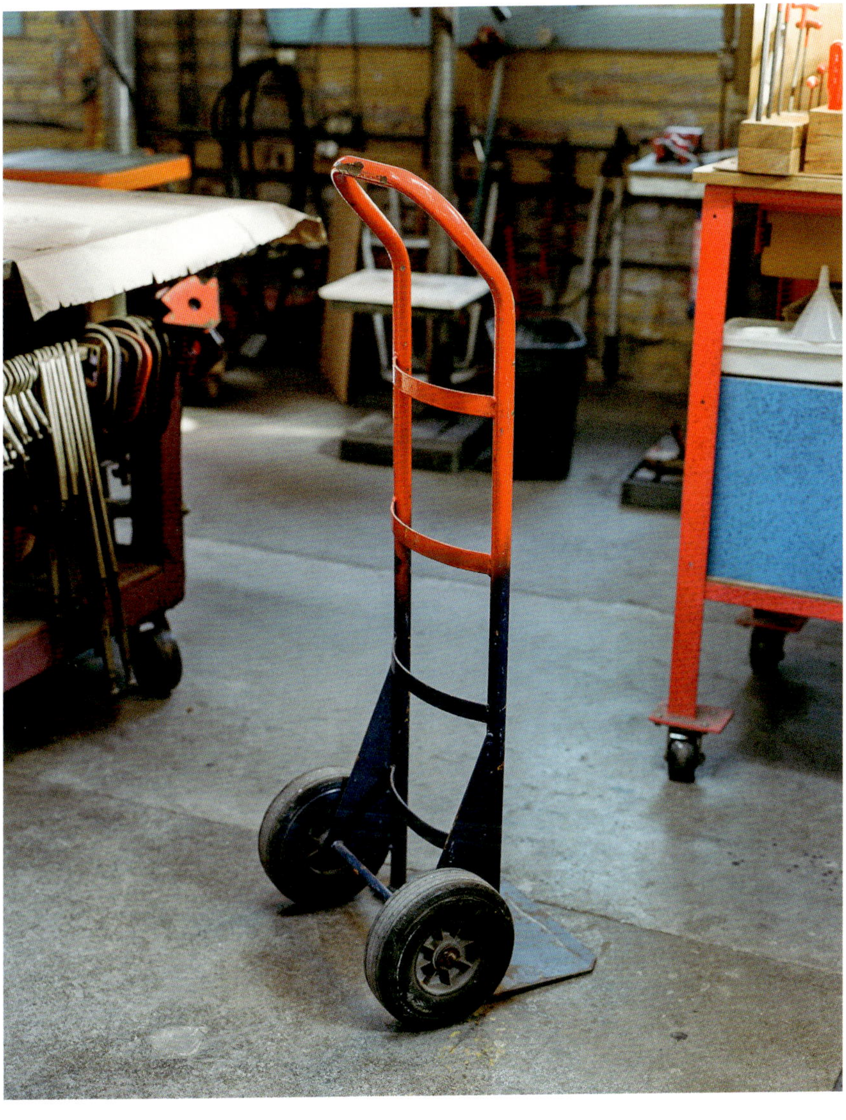

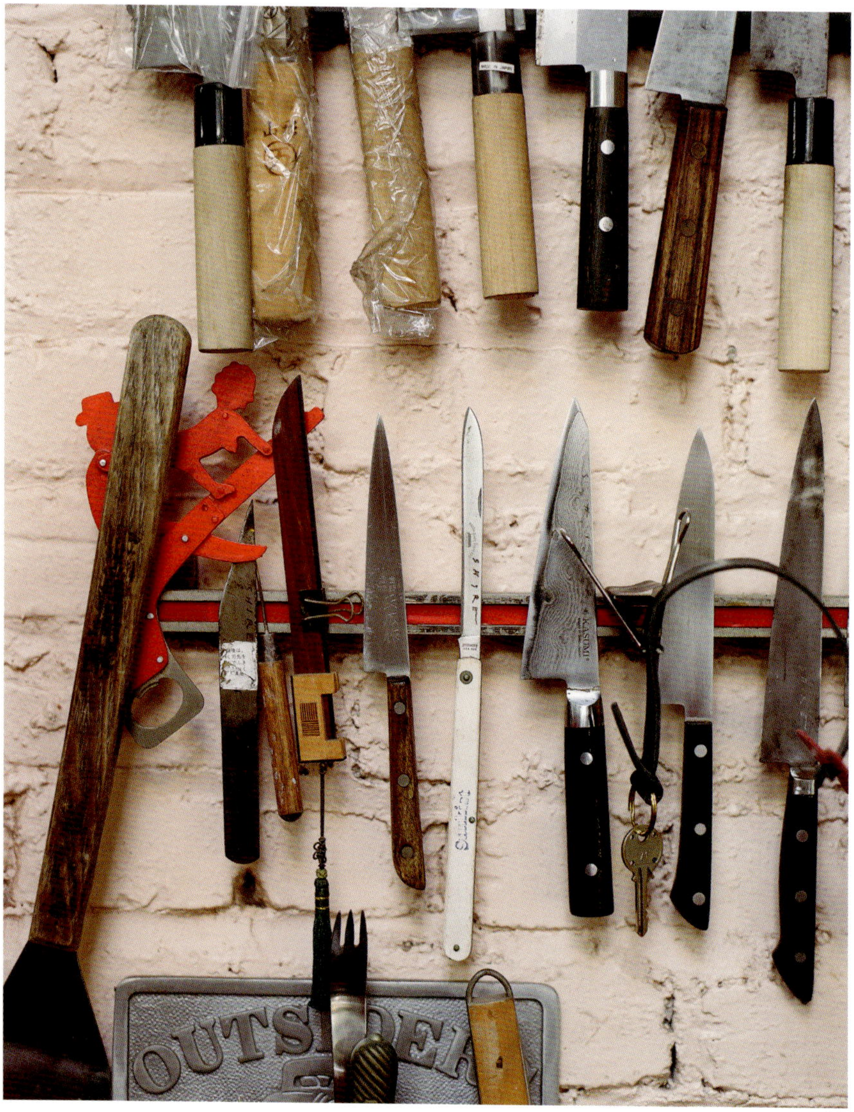

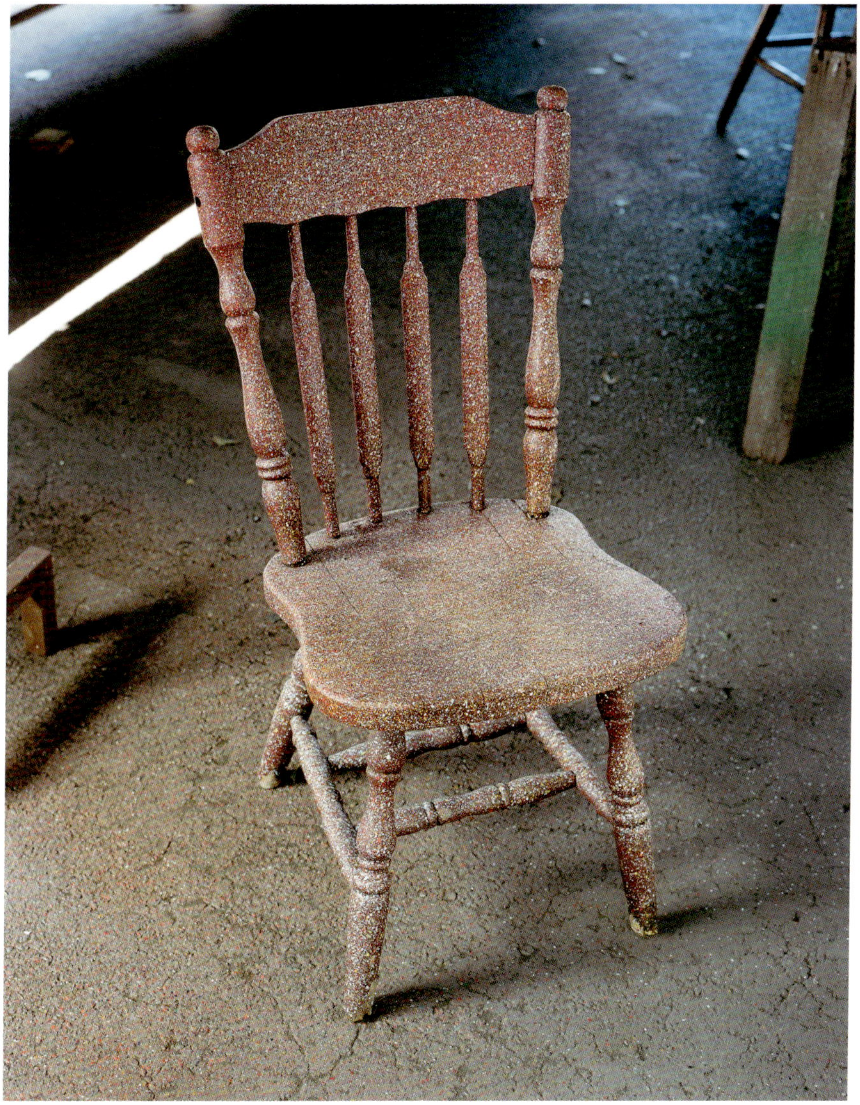

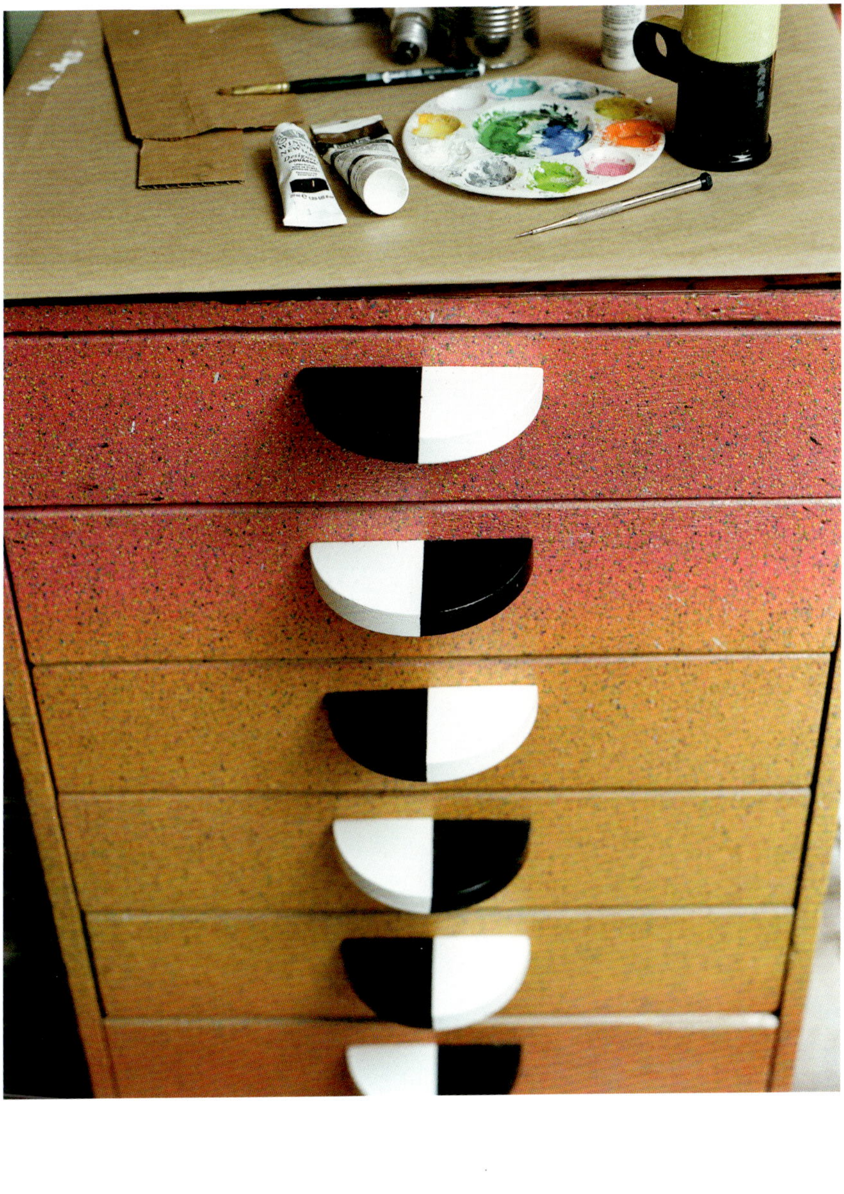

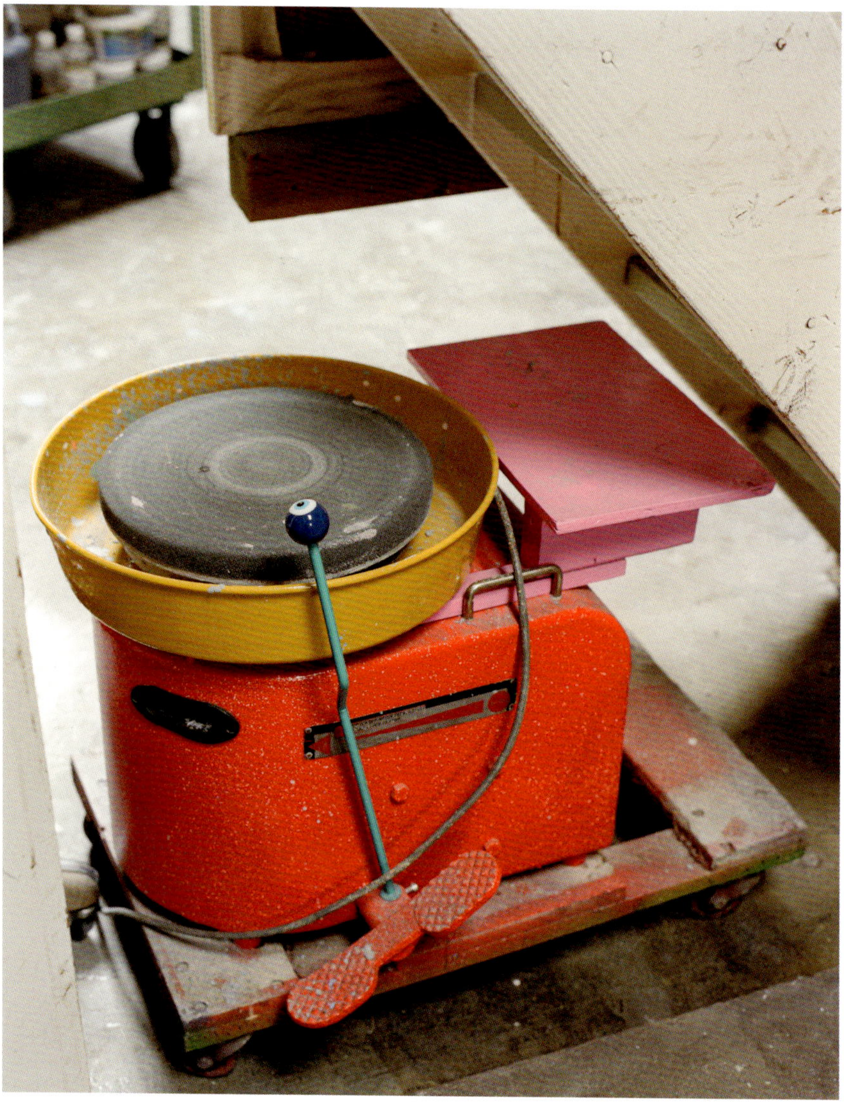

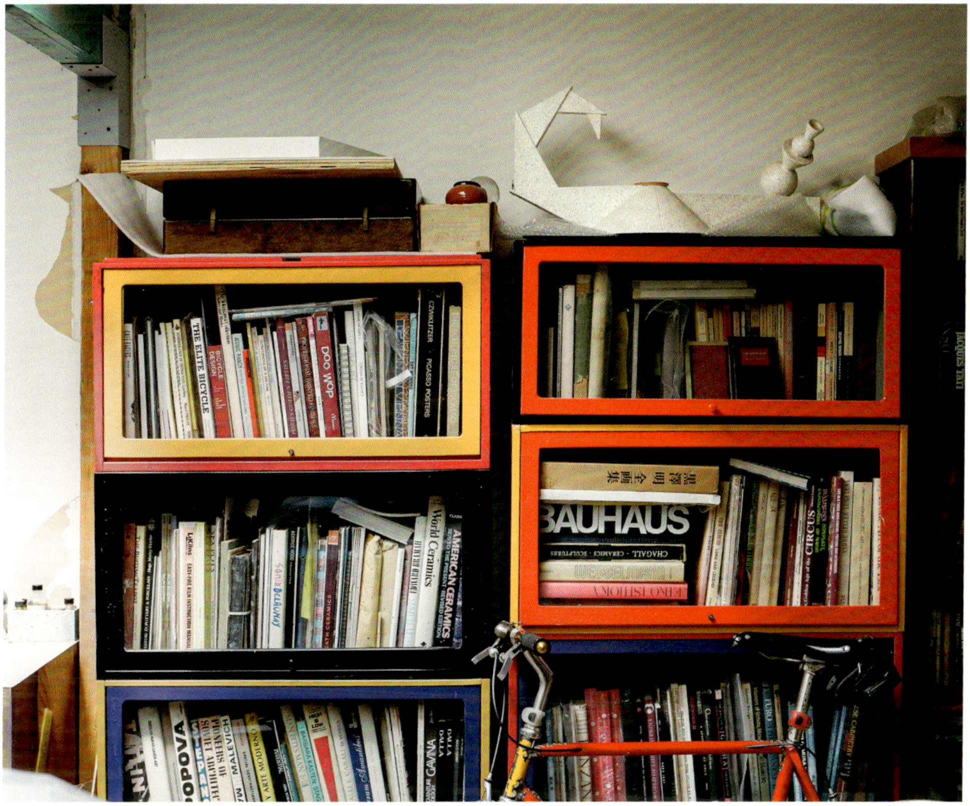
THE ELITE BICYCLE
BICYCLE DESIGN
DOO WOP
CZWIKLITZER
PICASSO POSTERS
JACQUES TATI
BAUHAUS
CHAGALL · CERAMICS · SCULPTURES
WESSELMANN
CIRCUS
AMERICAN CERAMICS
World Ceramics
POPOVA
MALEVICH
ARTE MODERNO
GAVINA

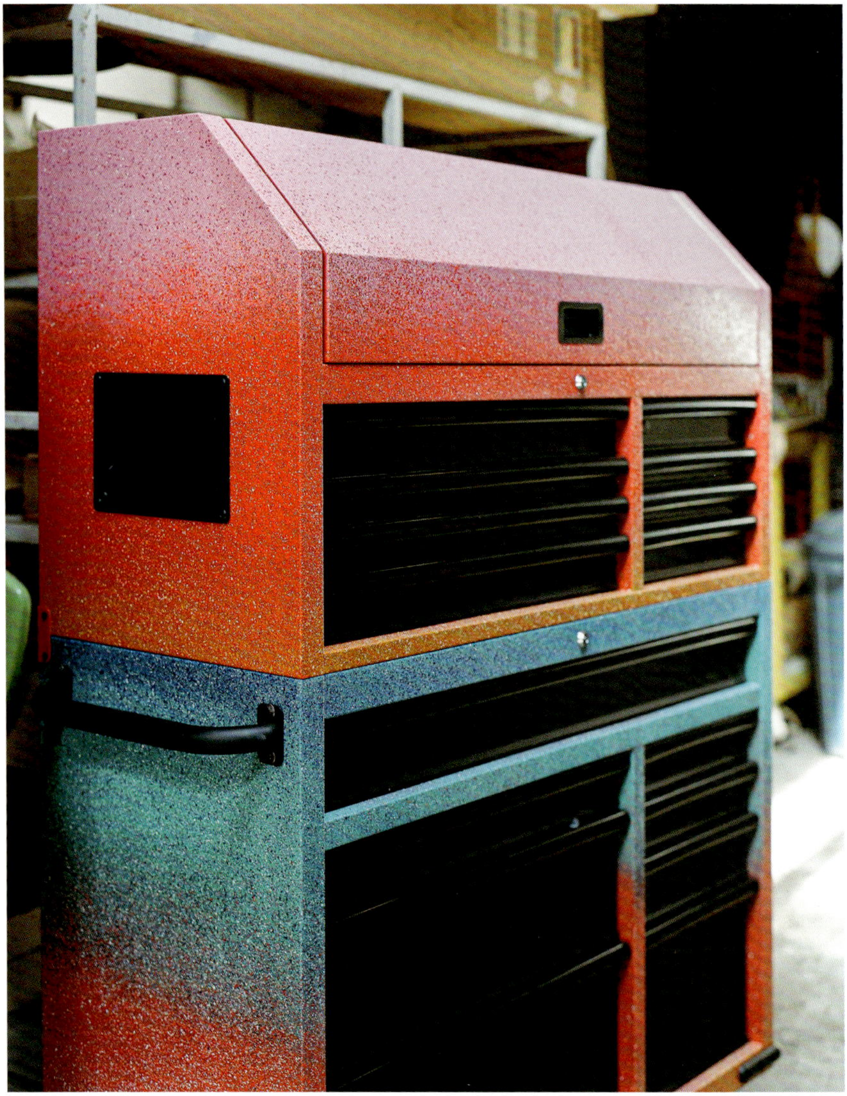

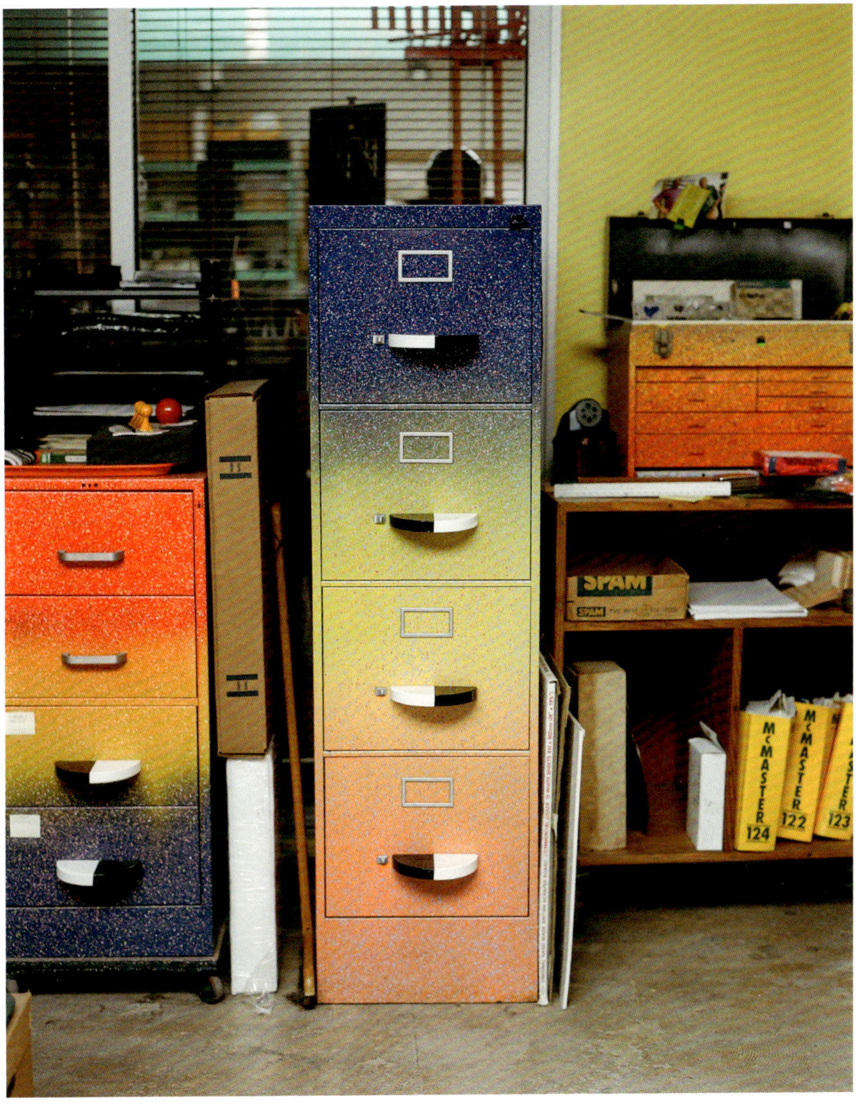
SPAM
McMASTER
124
McMASTER
122
123

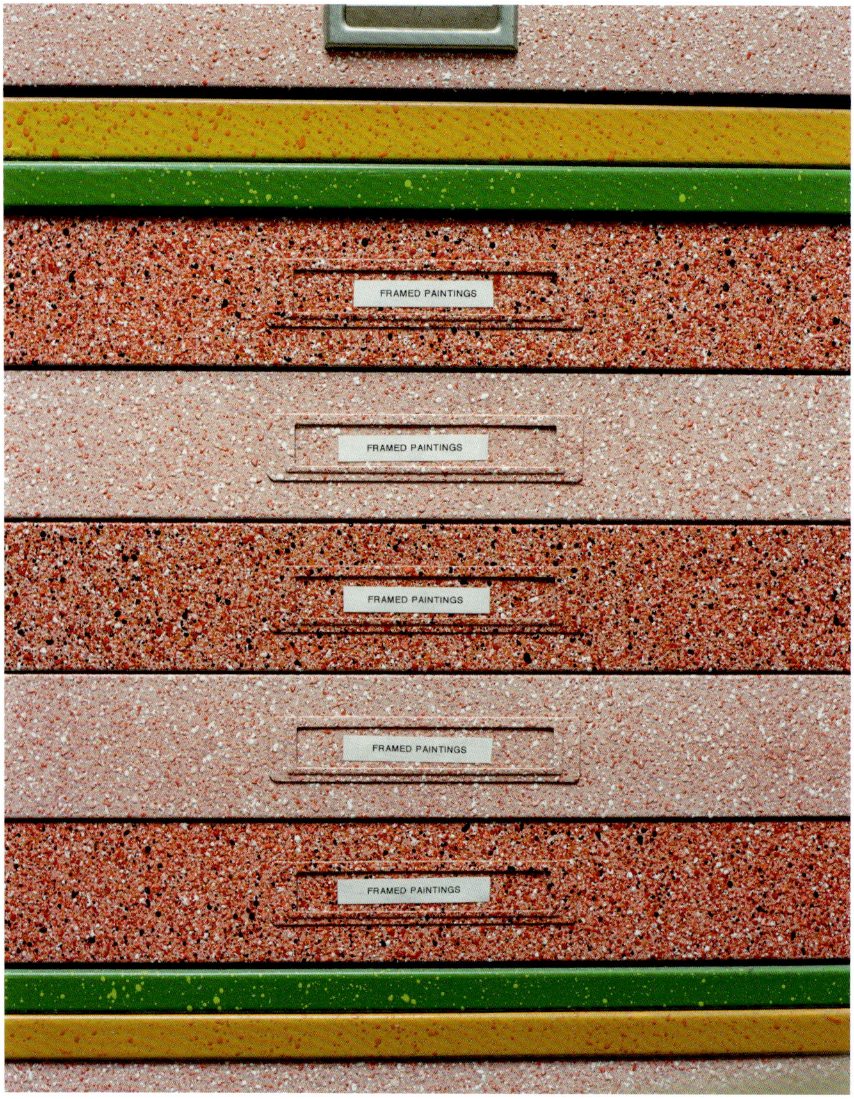
FRAMED PAINTINGS
FRAMED PAINTINGS
FRAMED PAINTINGS
FRAMED PAINTINGS
FRAMED PAINTINGS

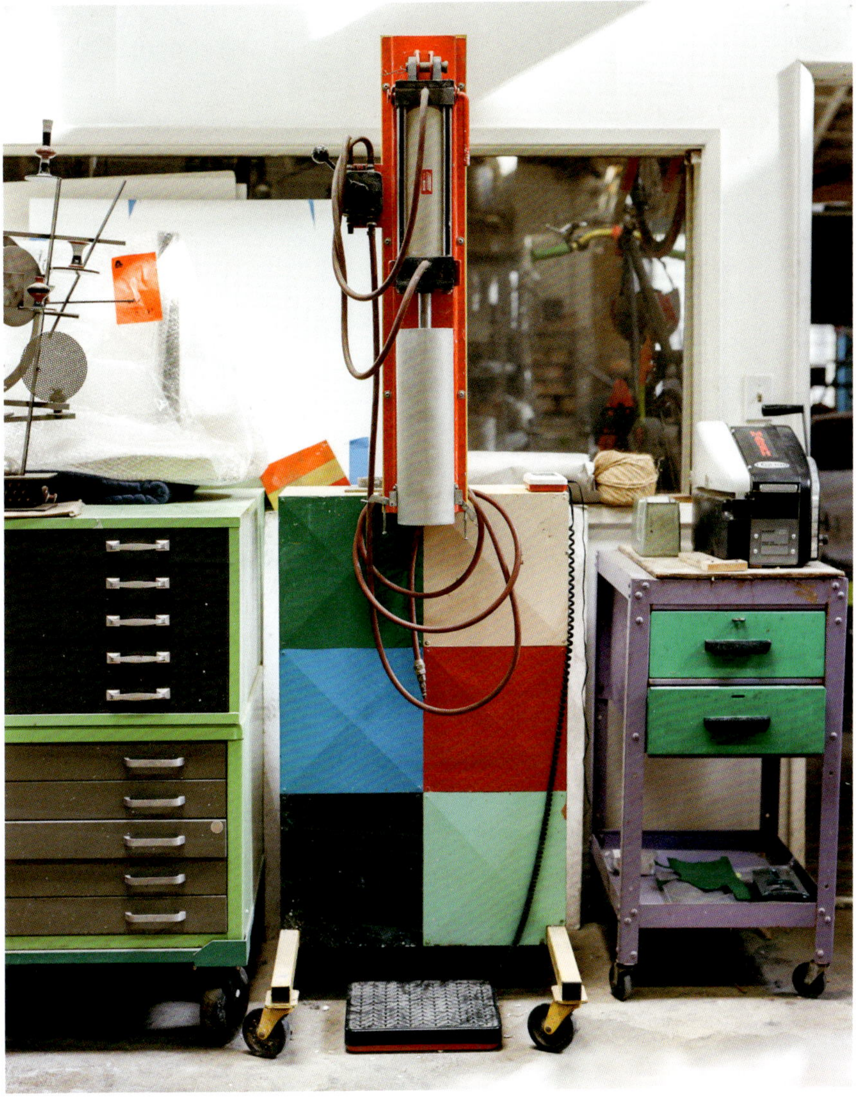

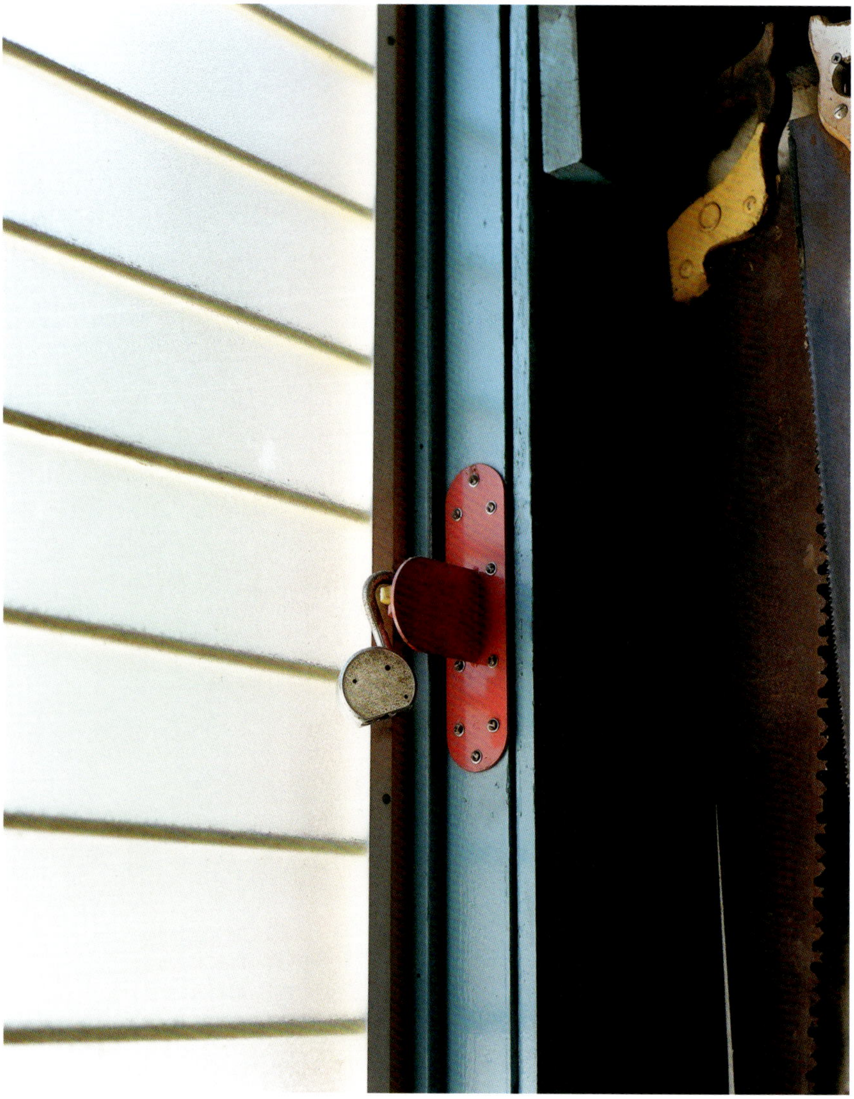

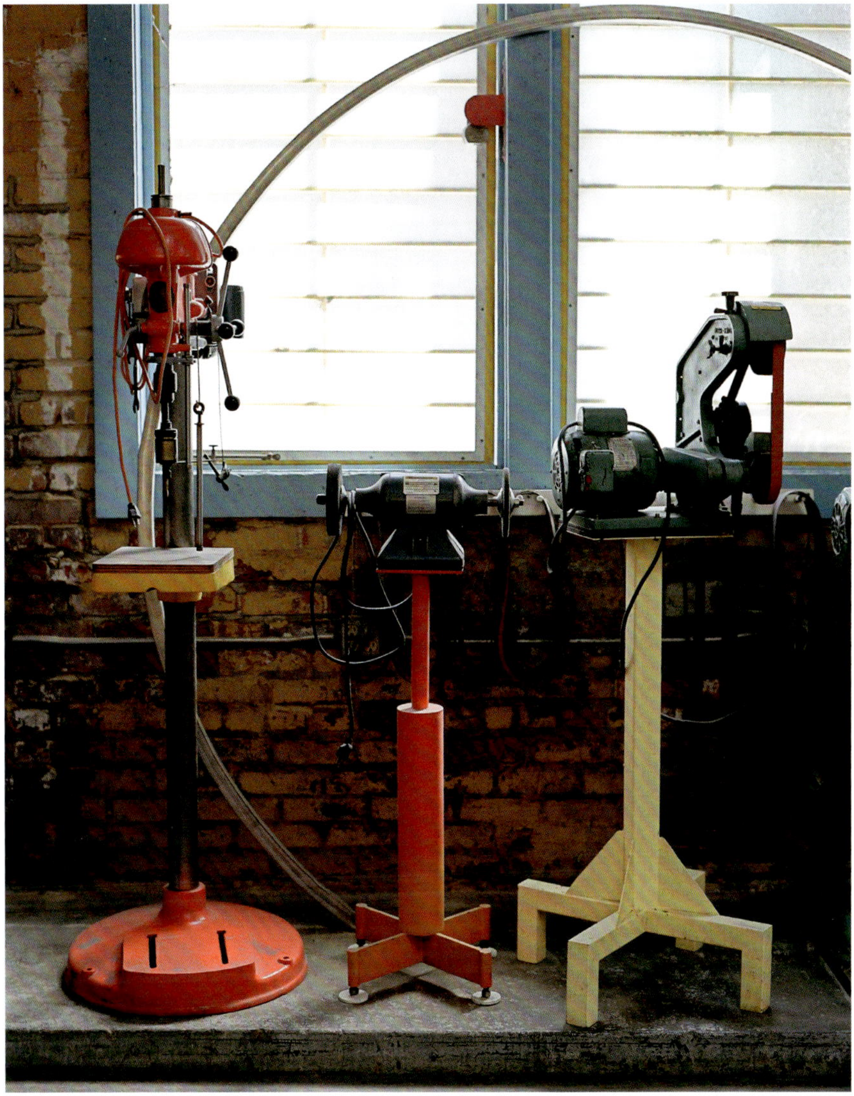

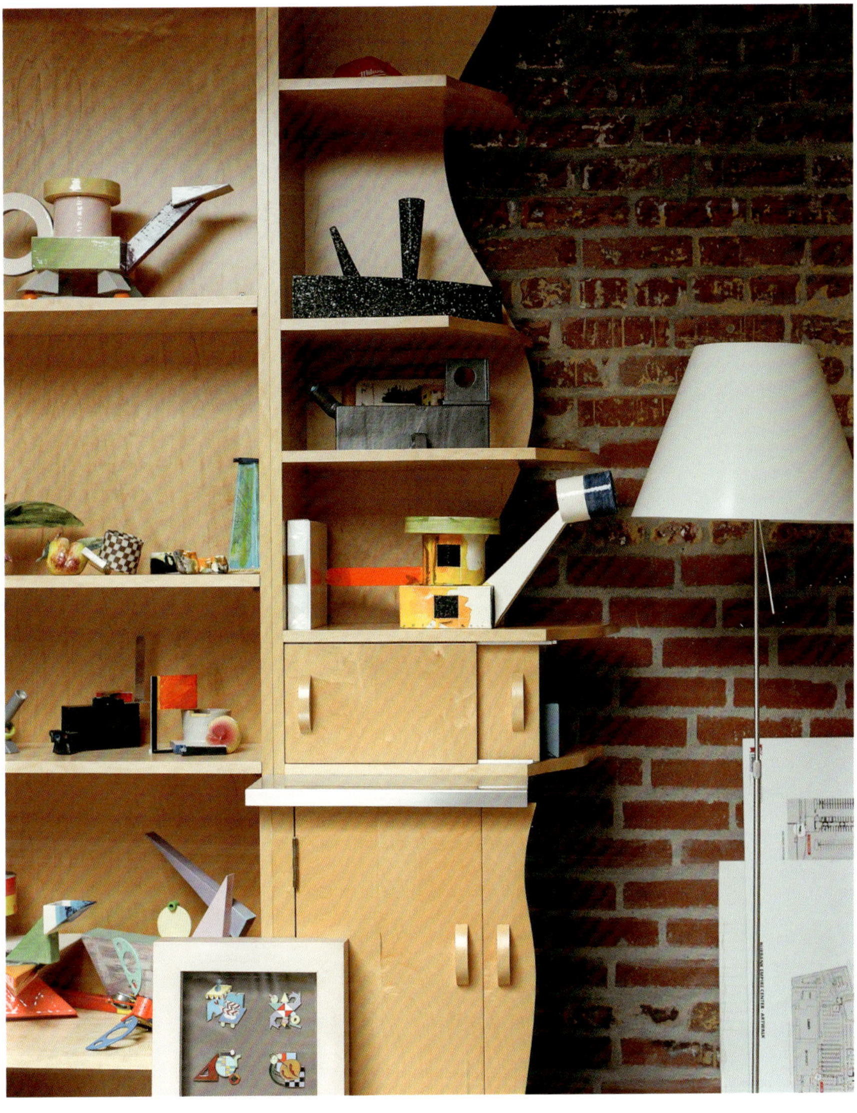

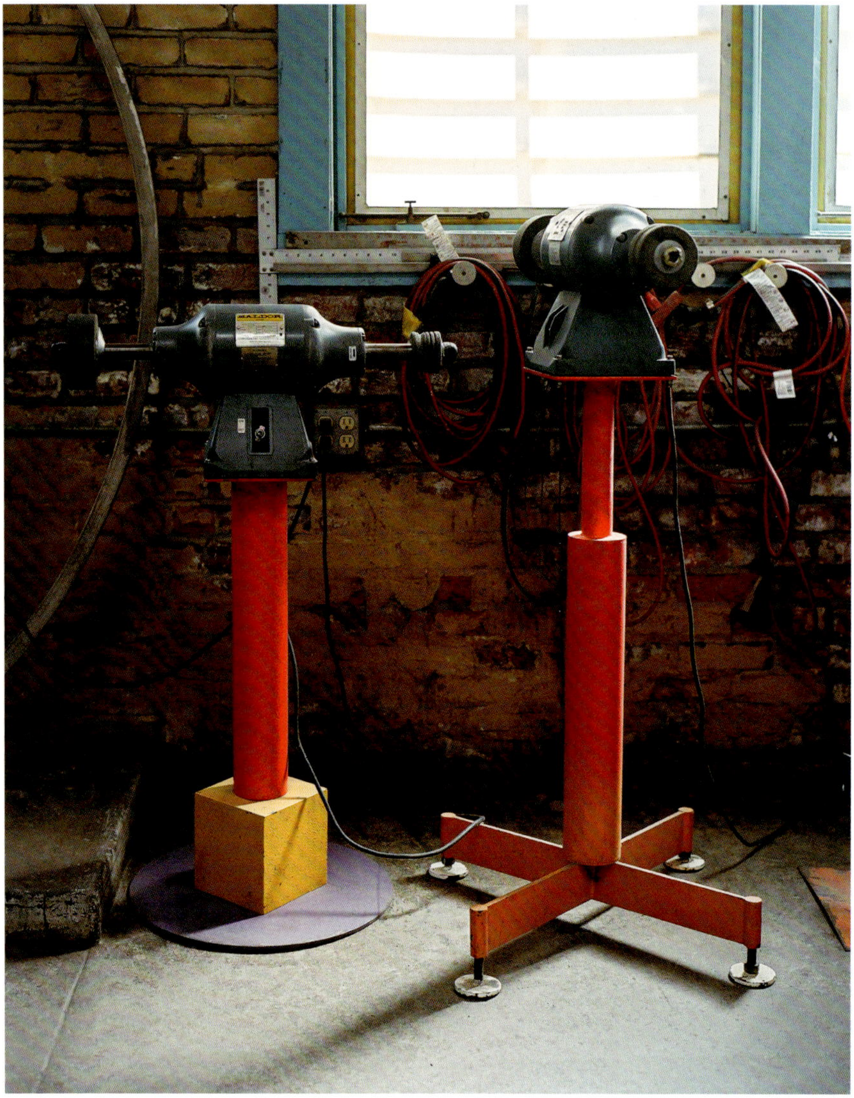

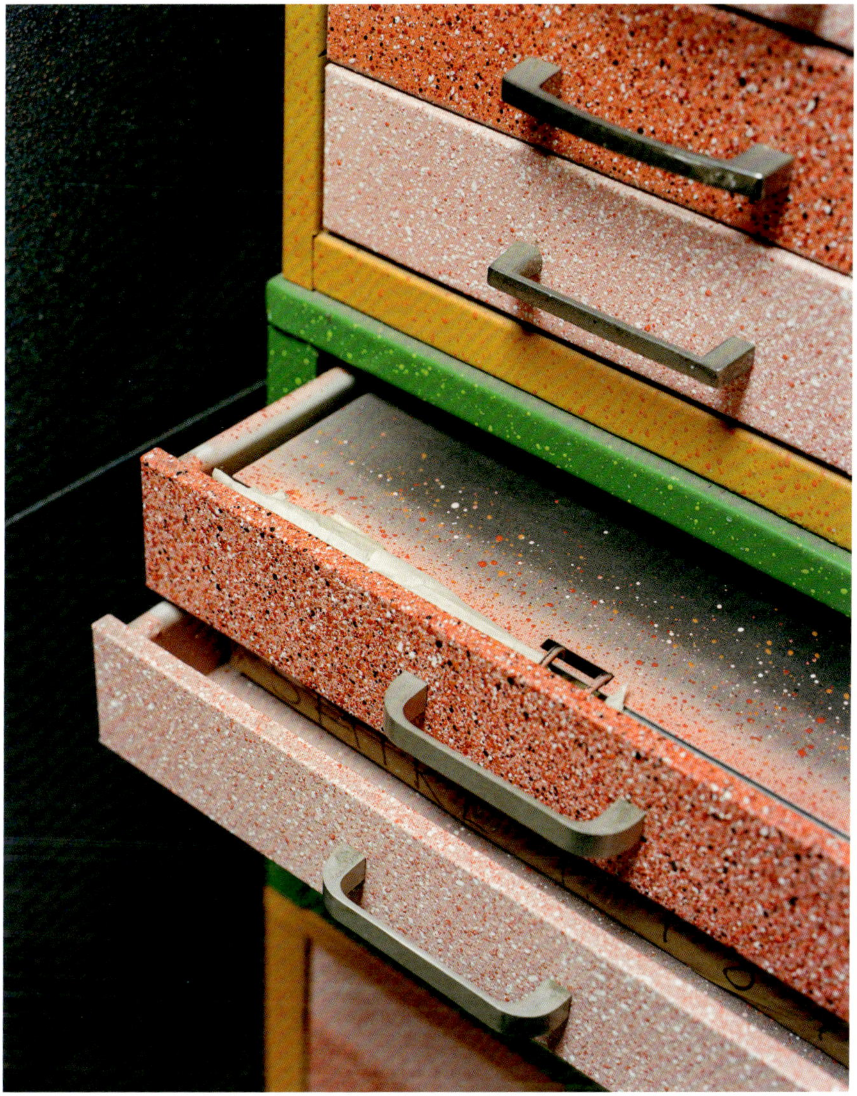

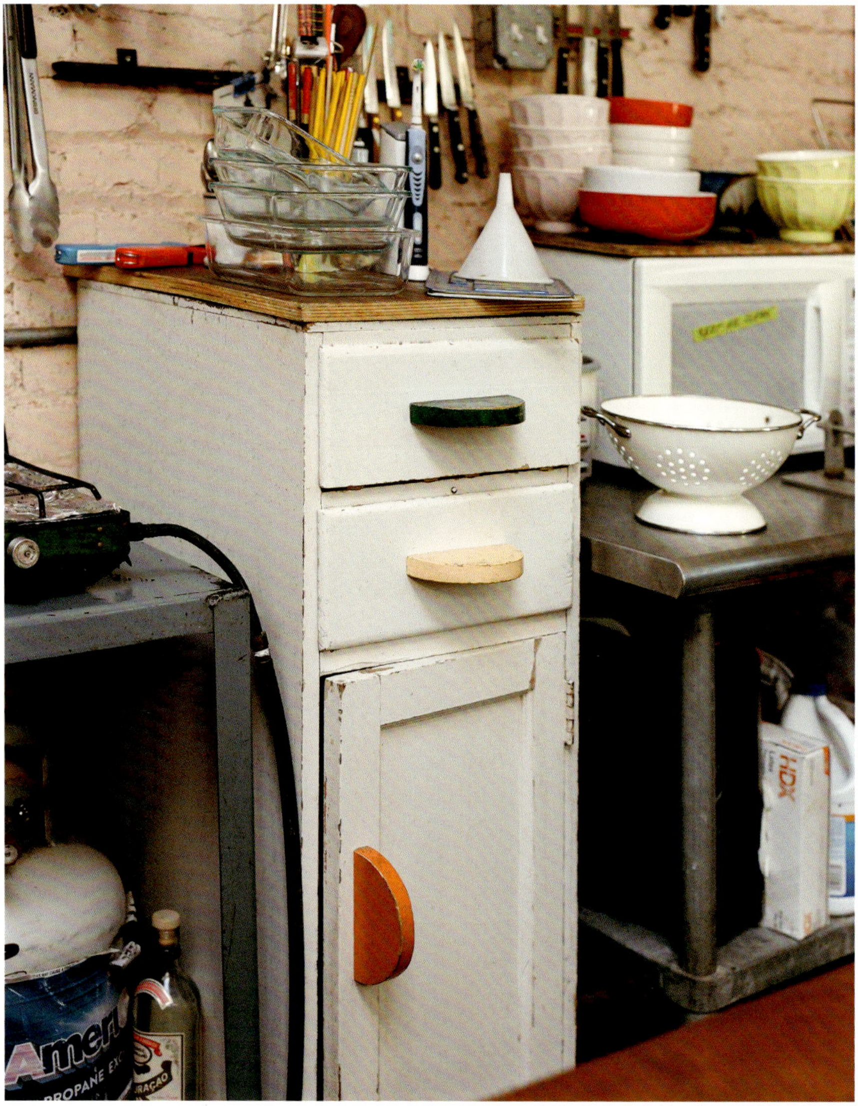

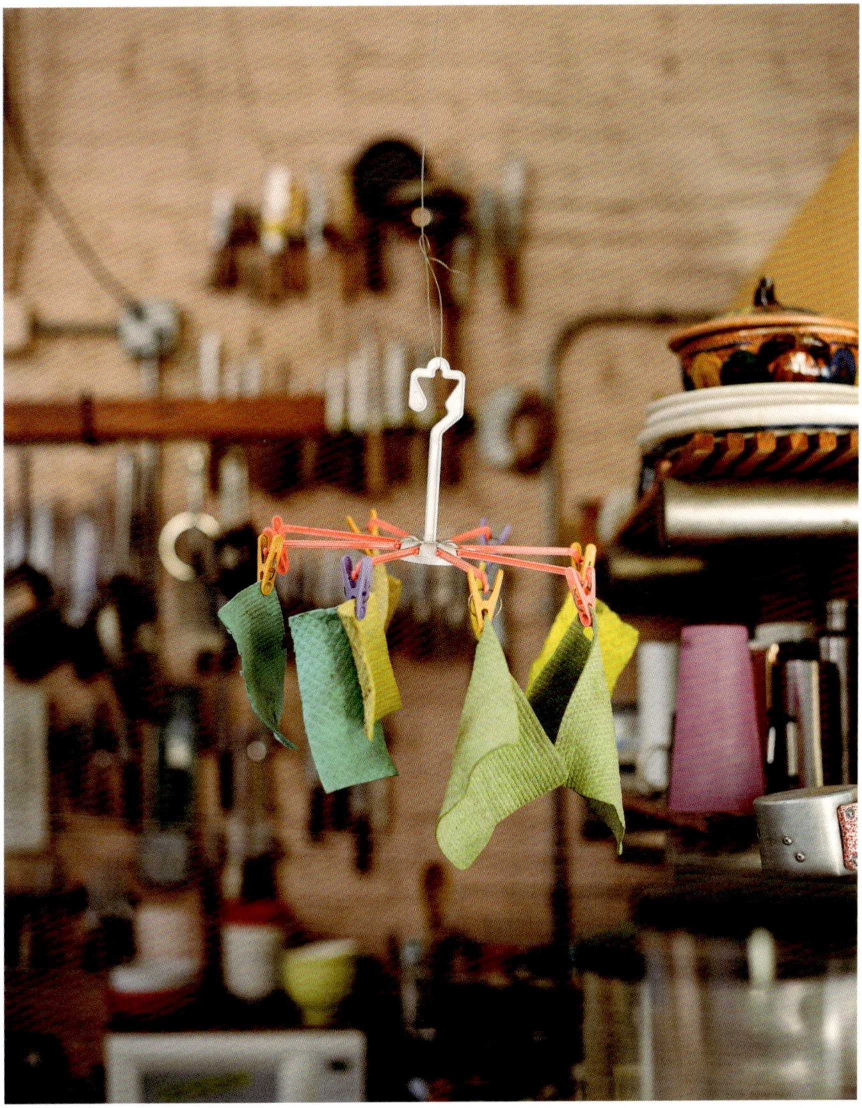

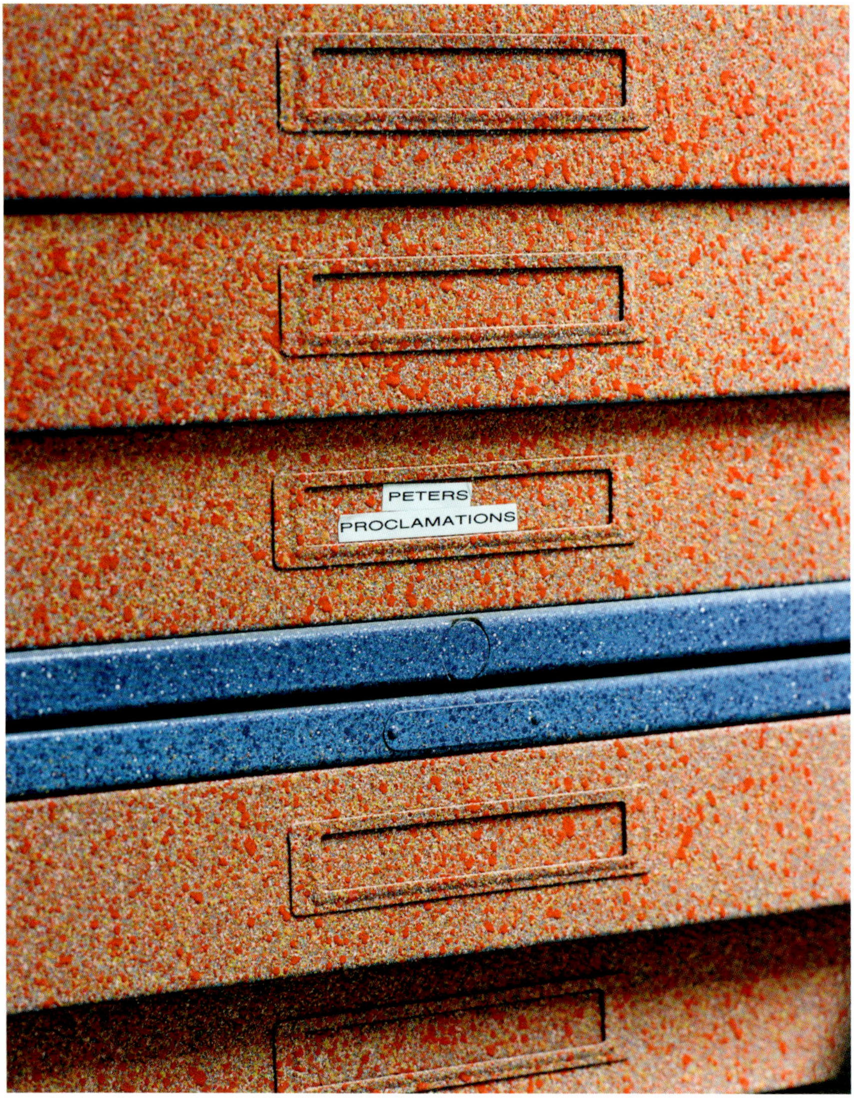
PETERS
PROCLAMATIONS

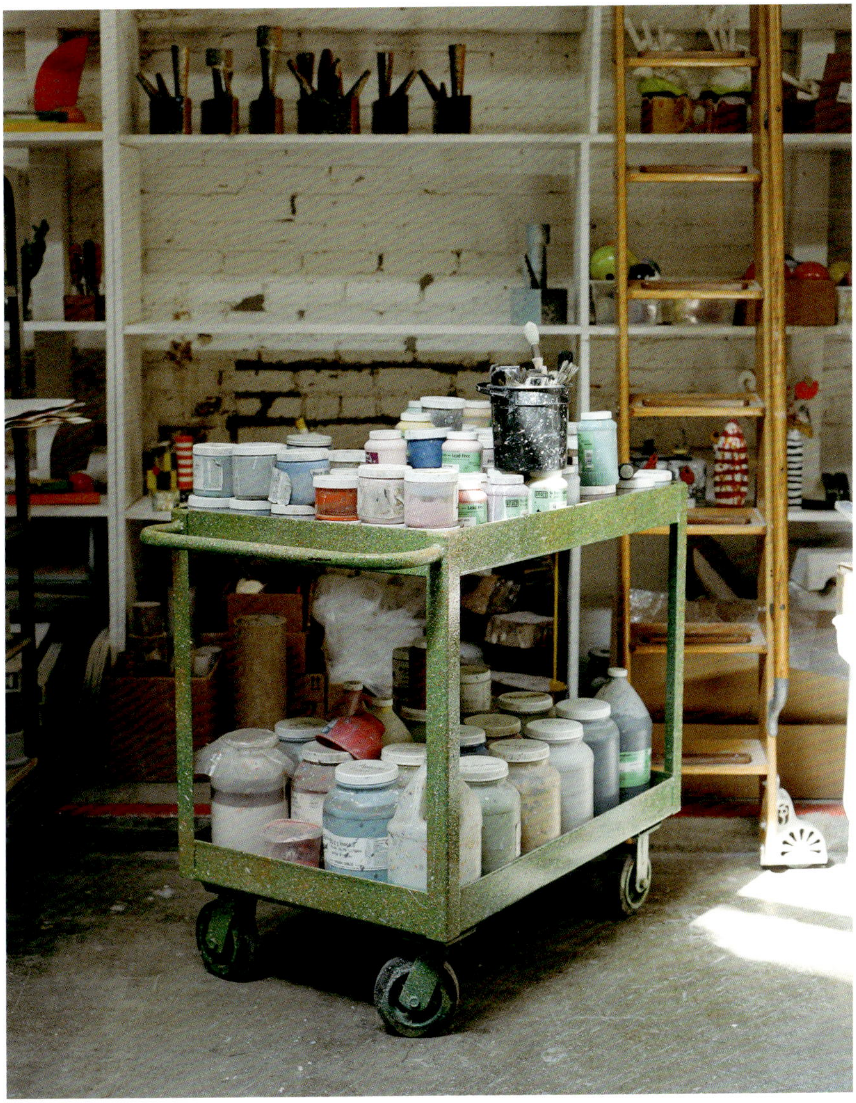

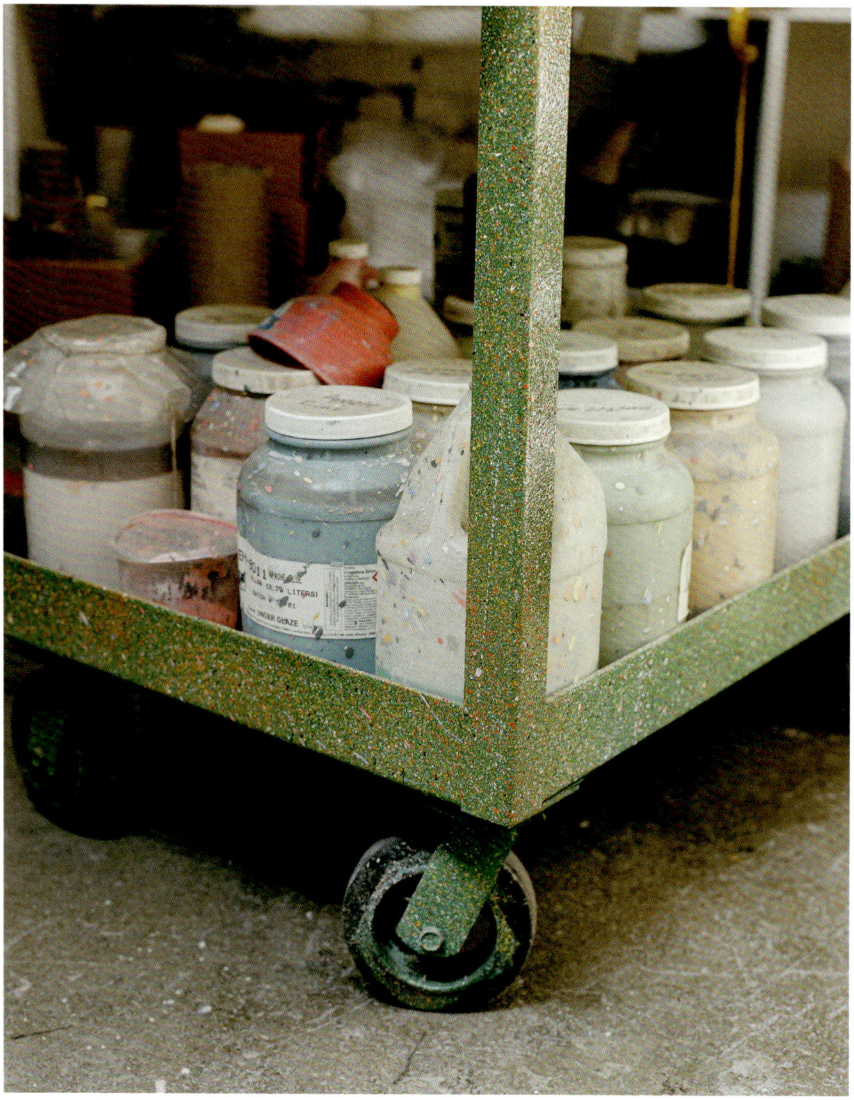
UNDER GLAZE

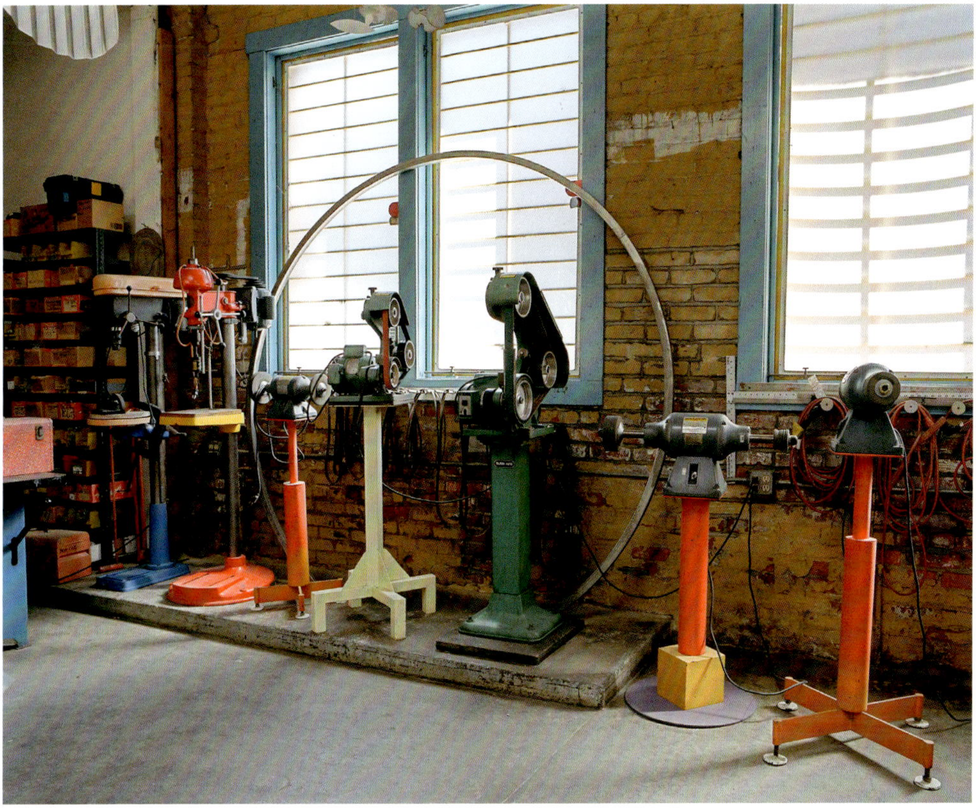

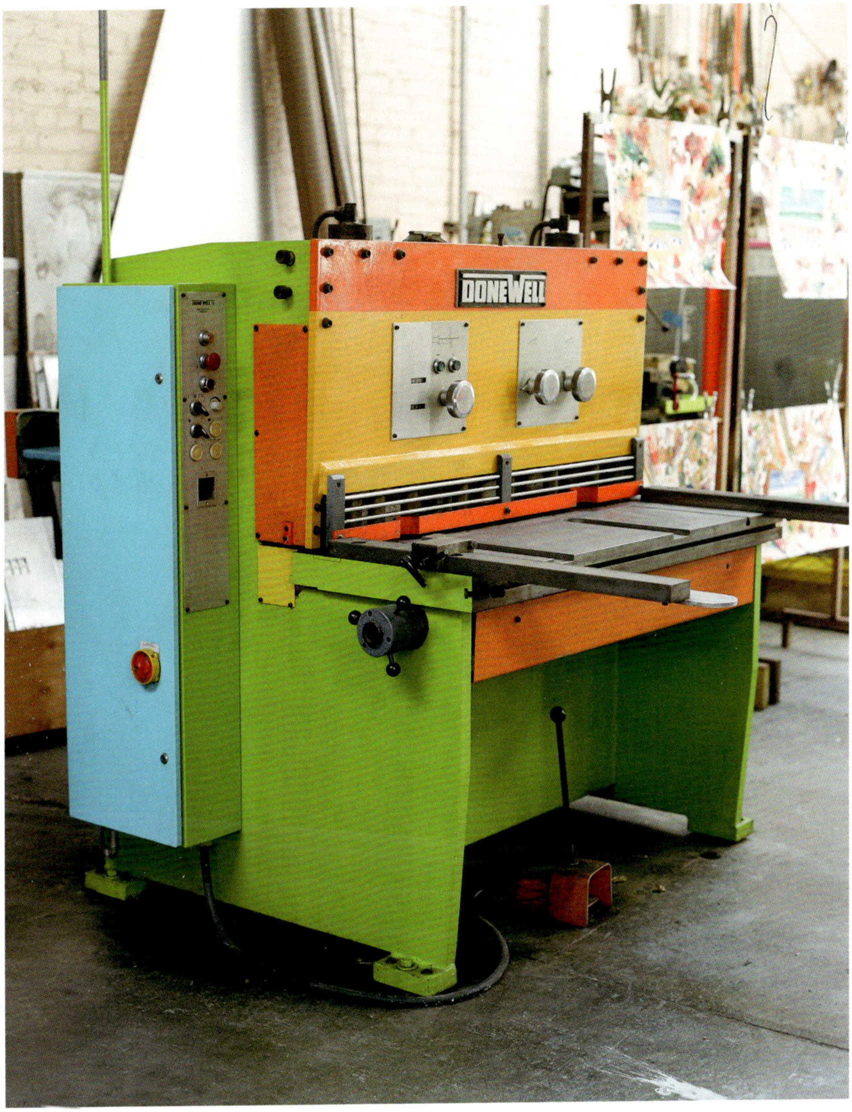
DONEWELL

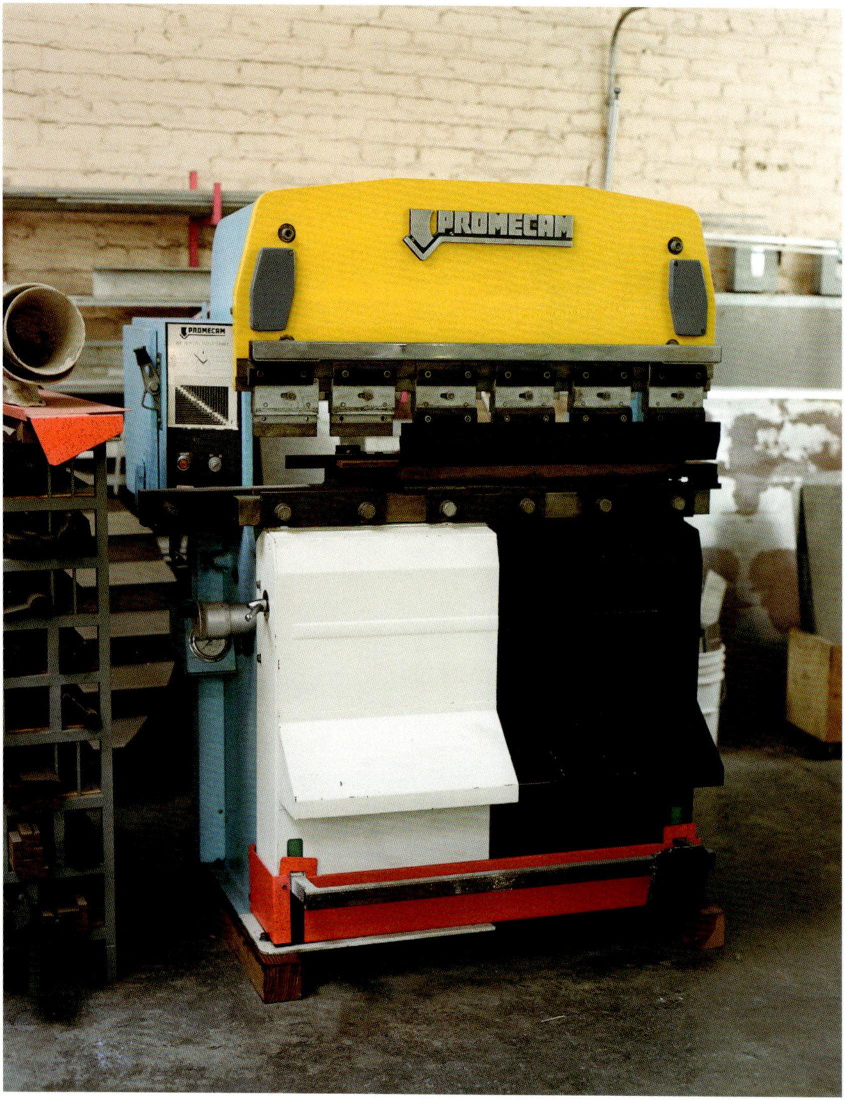
PROMECAM
PROMECAM

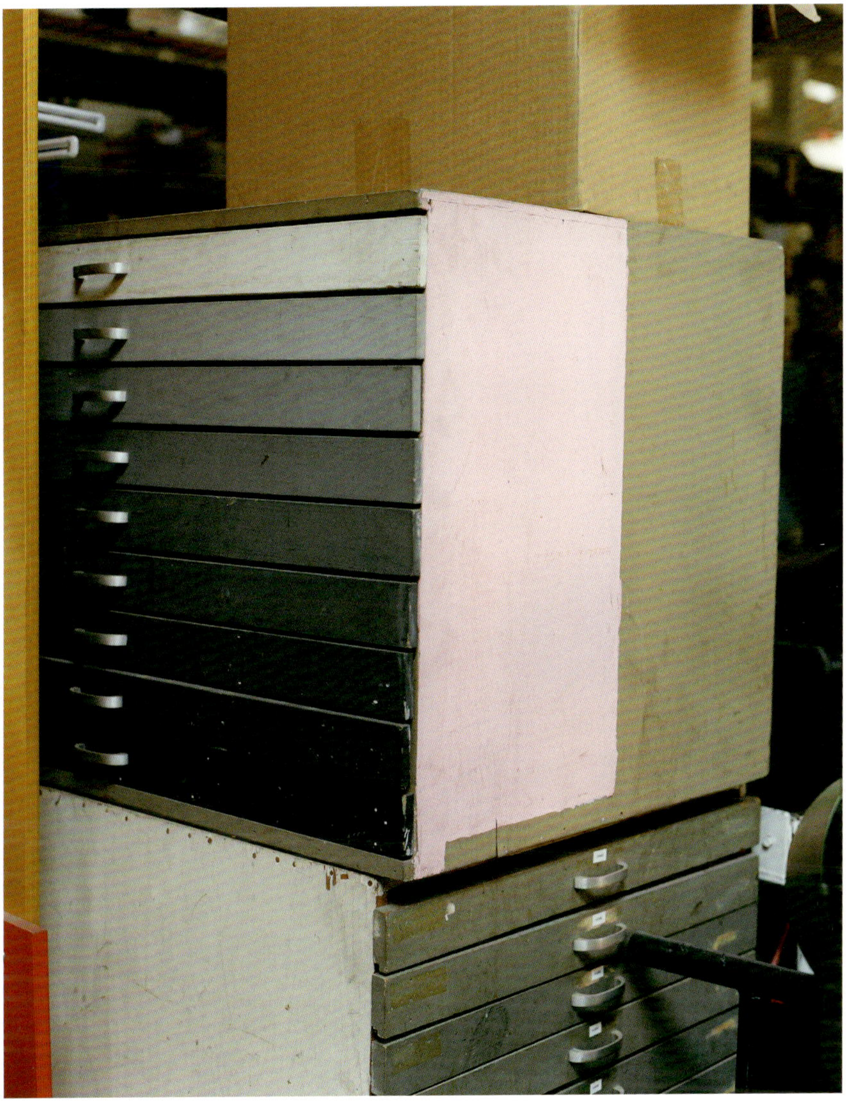

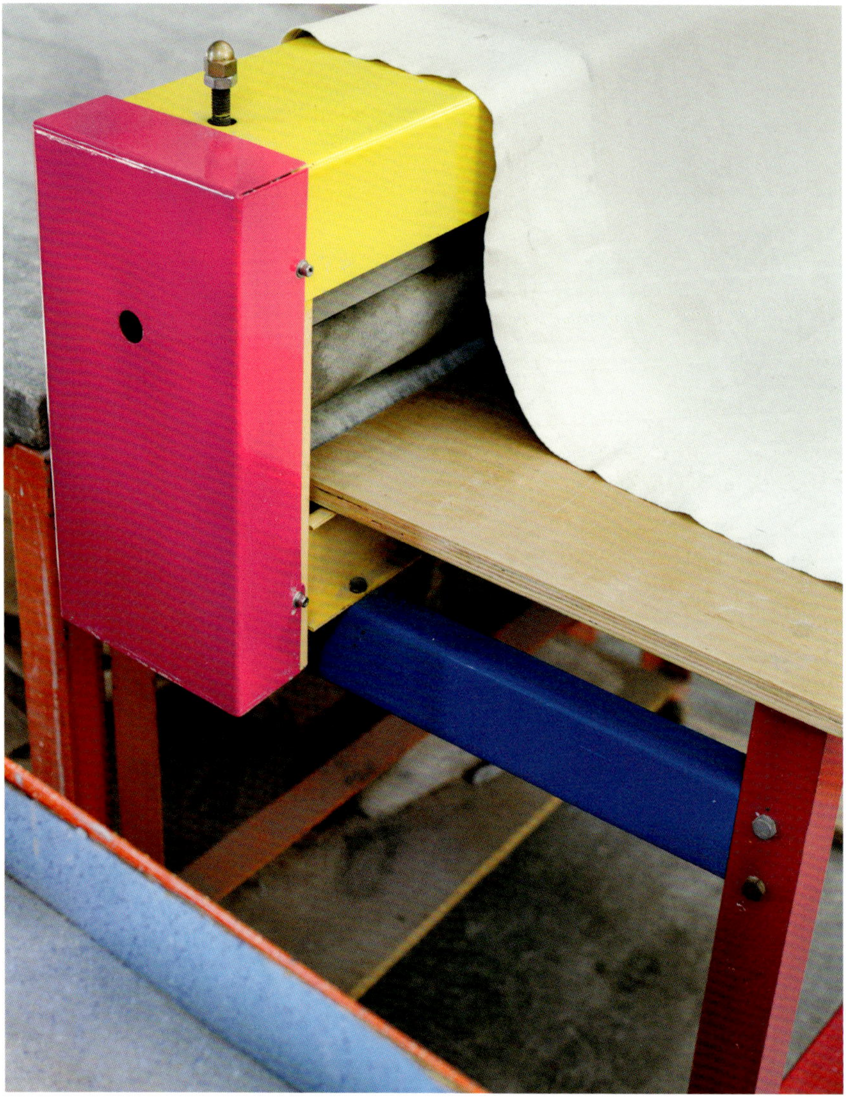

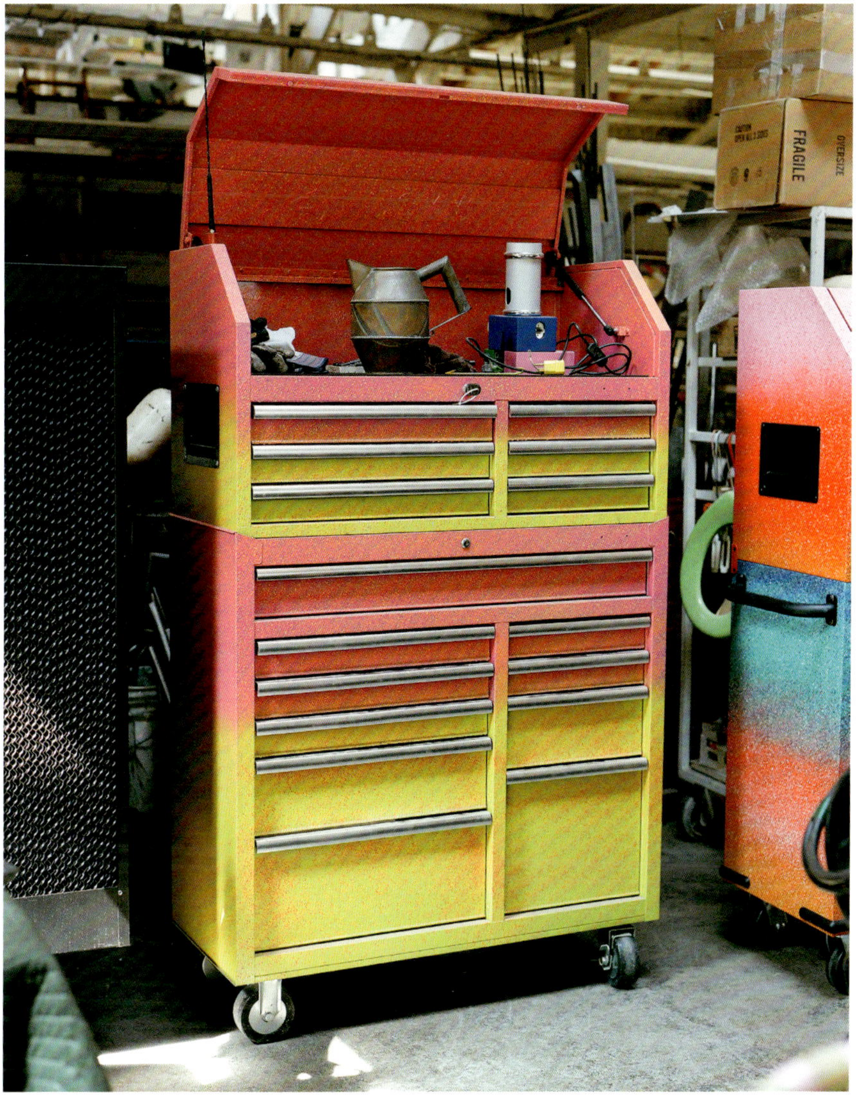
FRAGILE
OVERSIZE

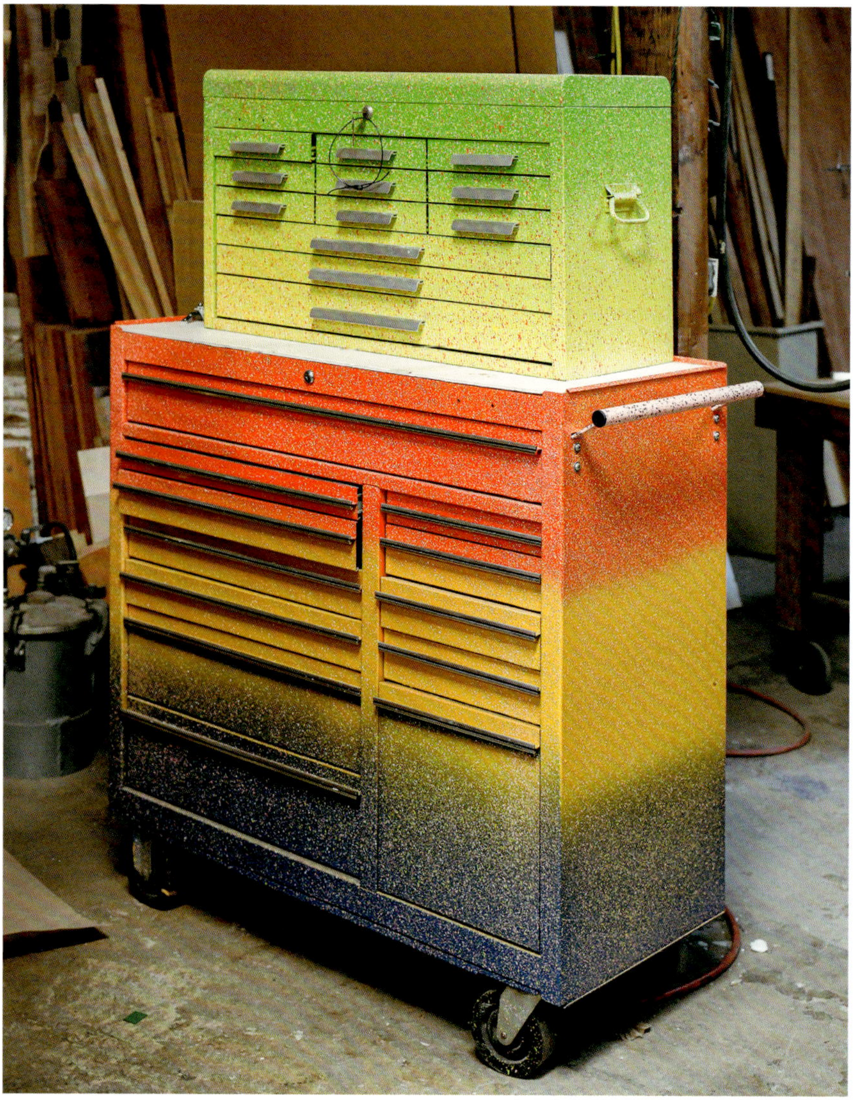

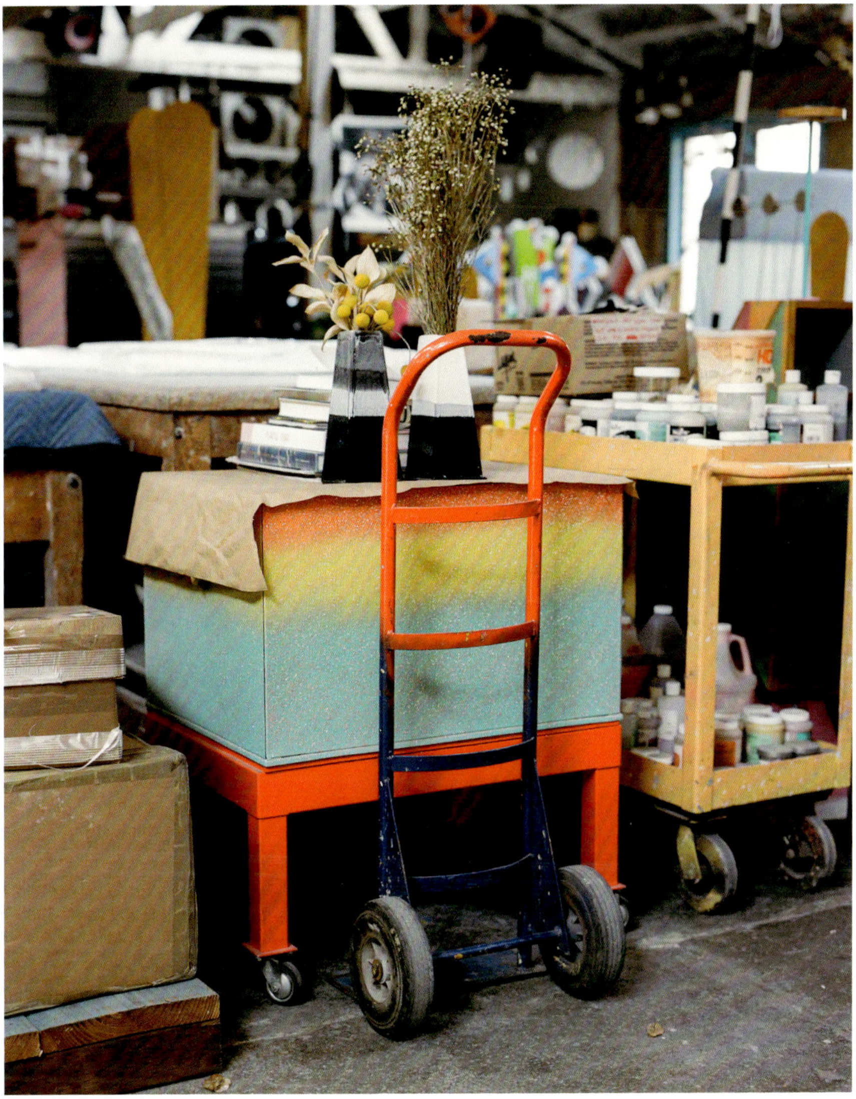

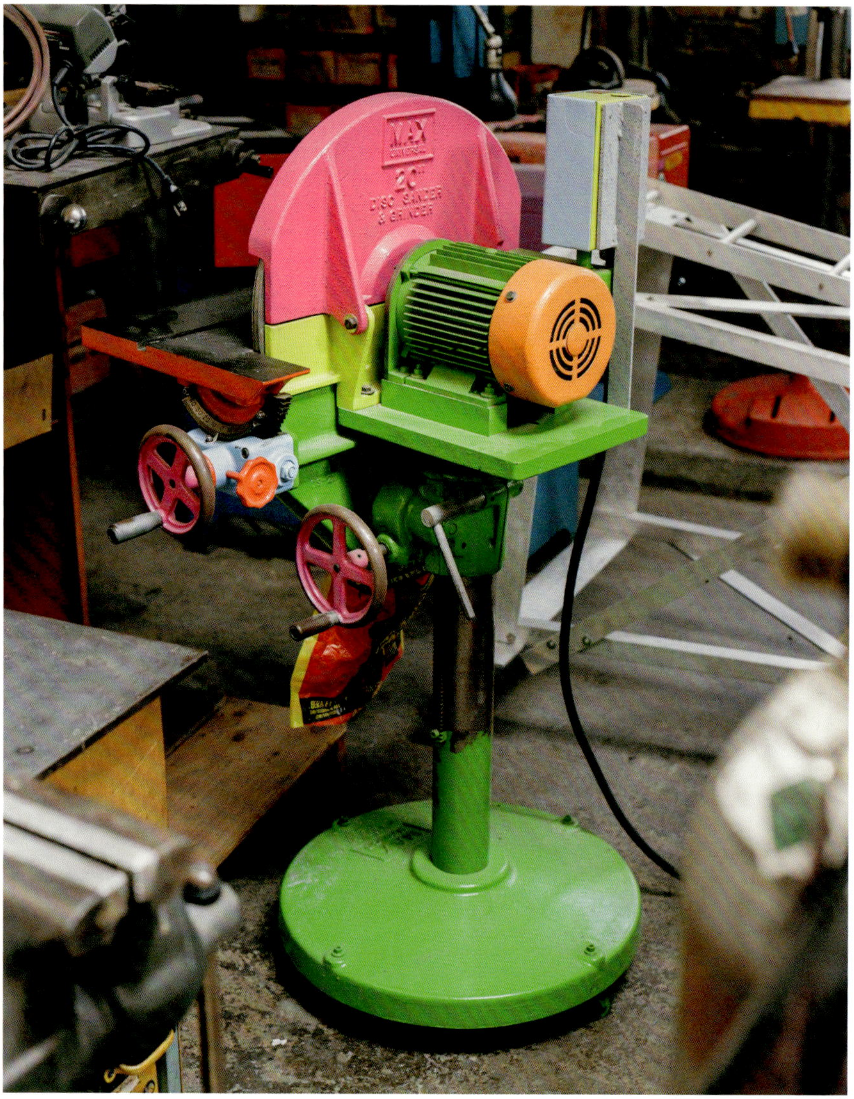
MAX
20"
DISC SANDER
& GRINDER

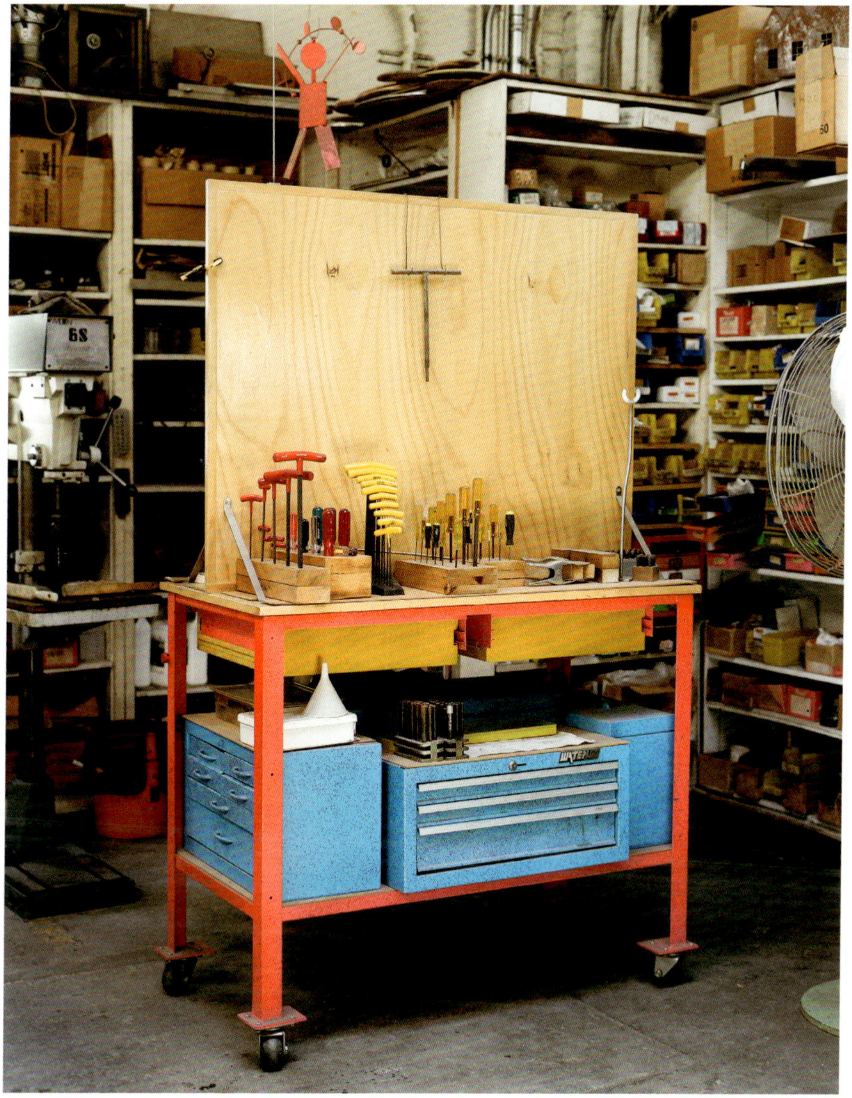

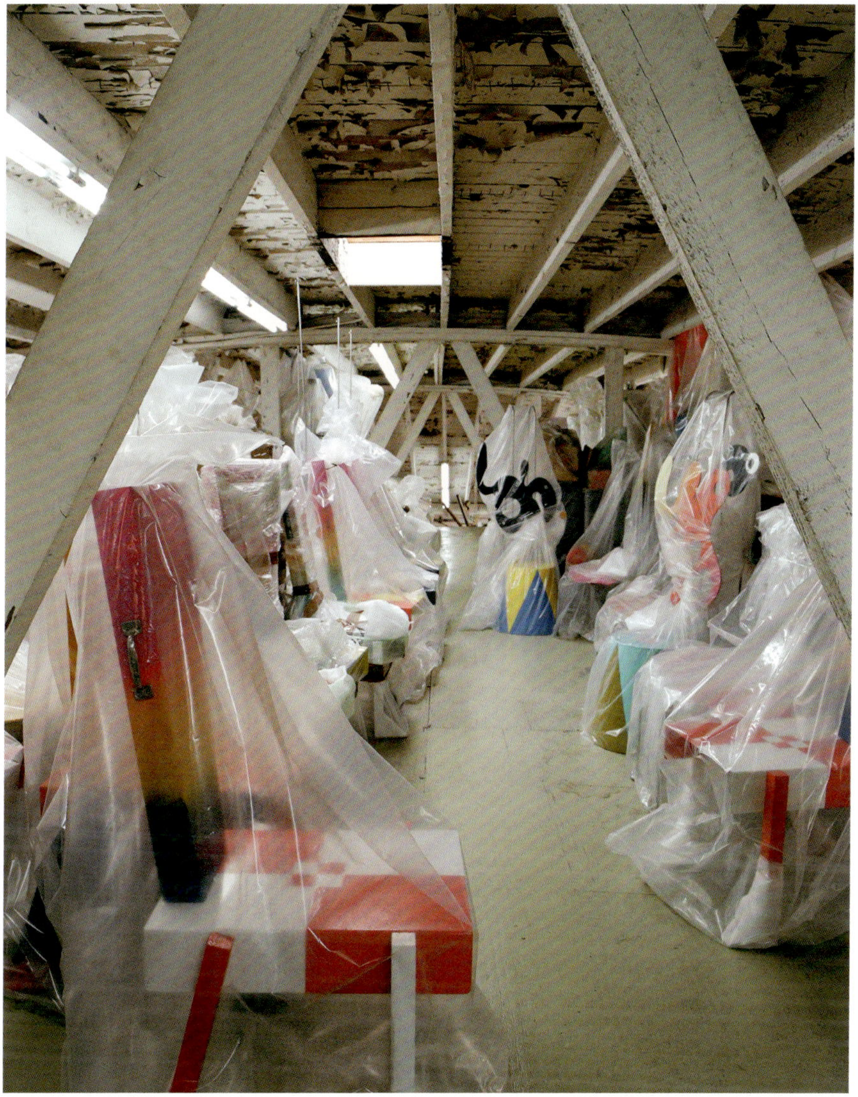

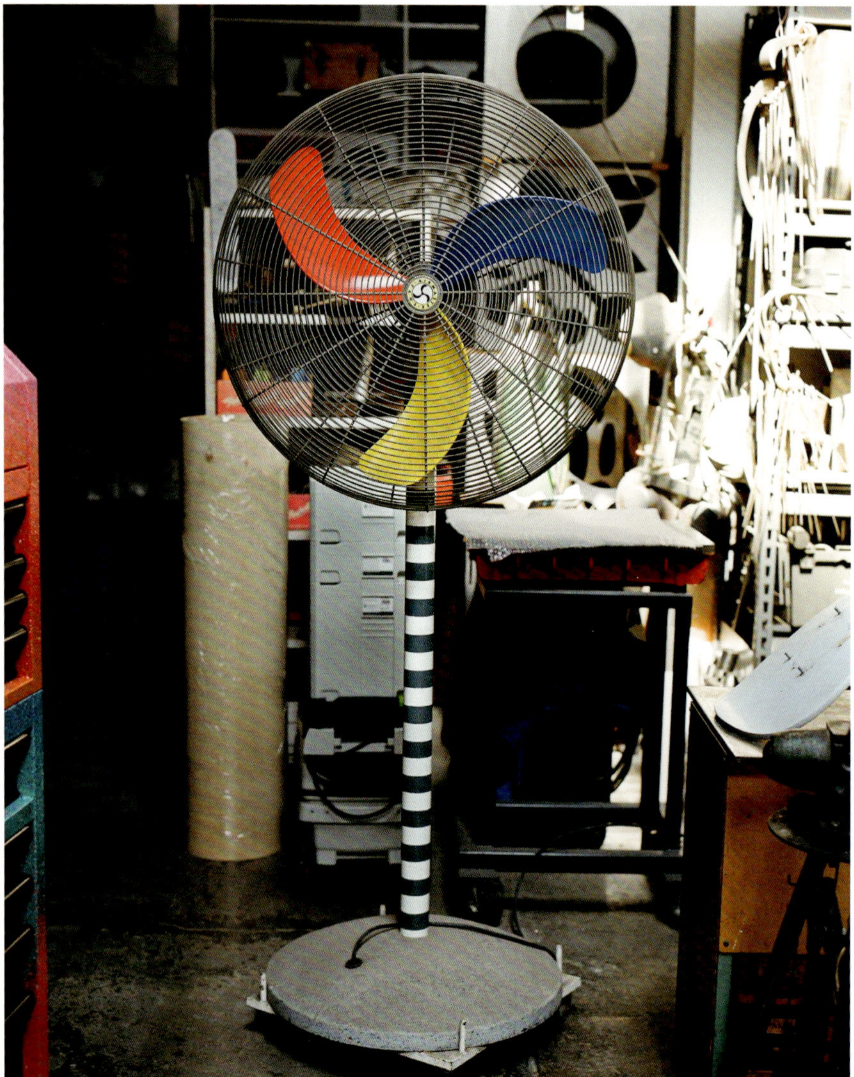

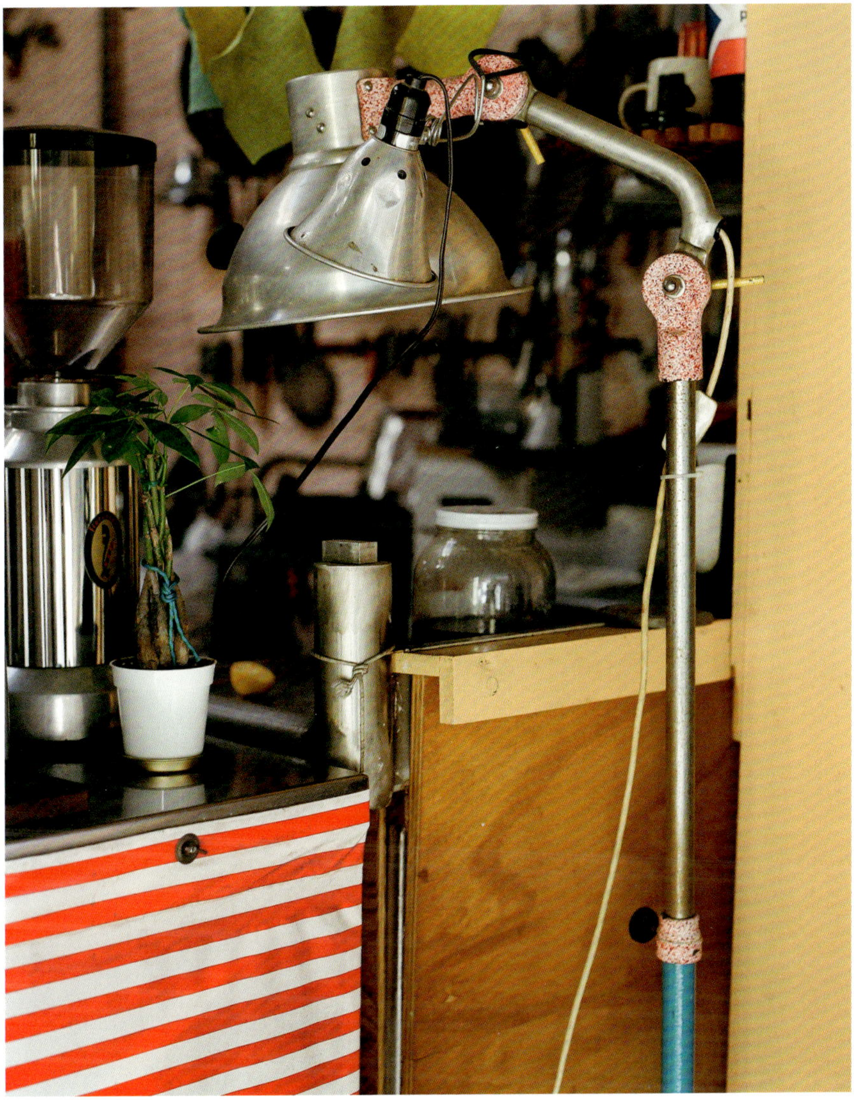

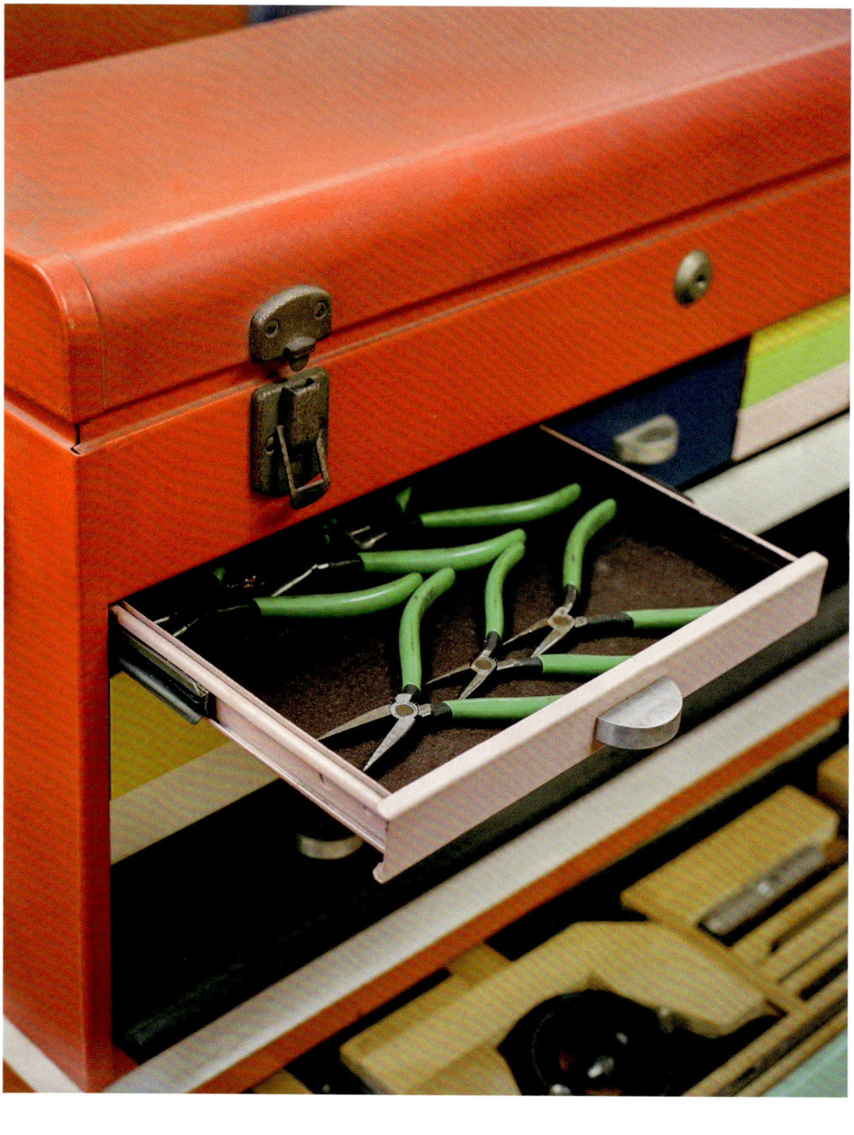

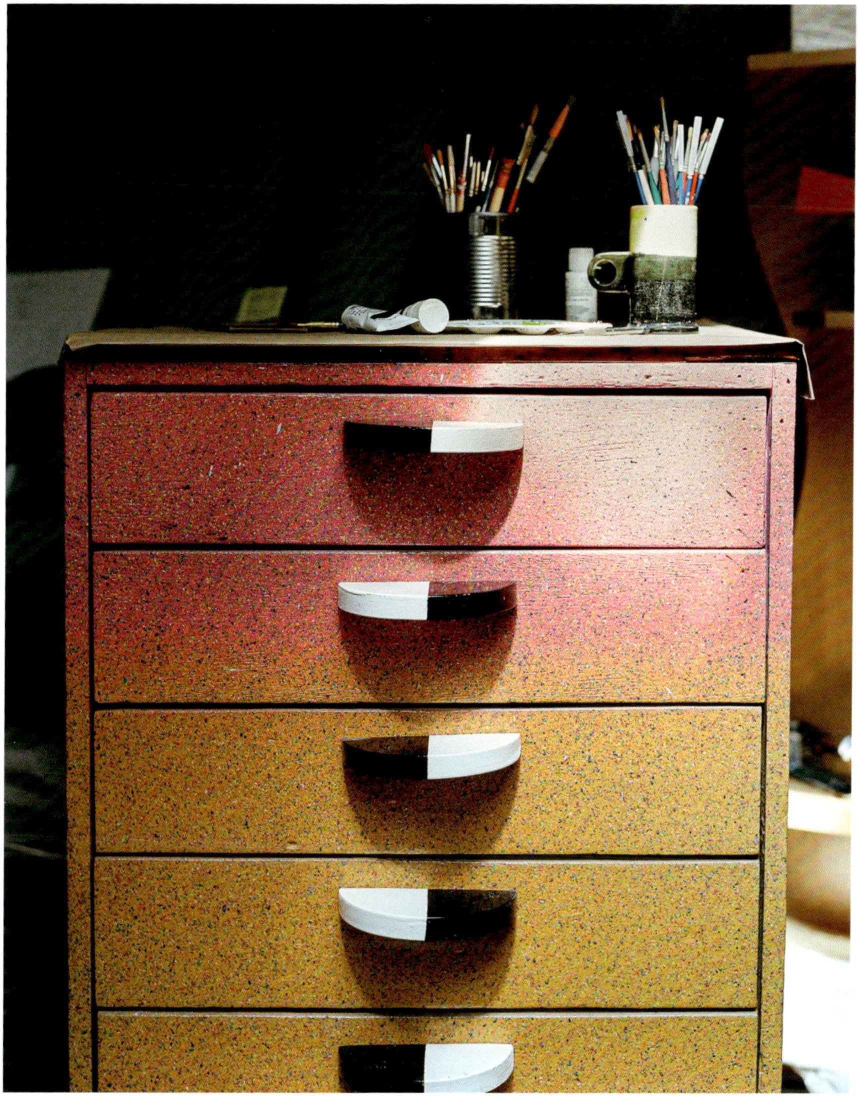

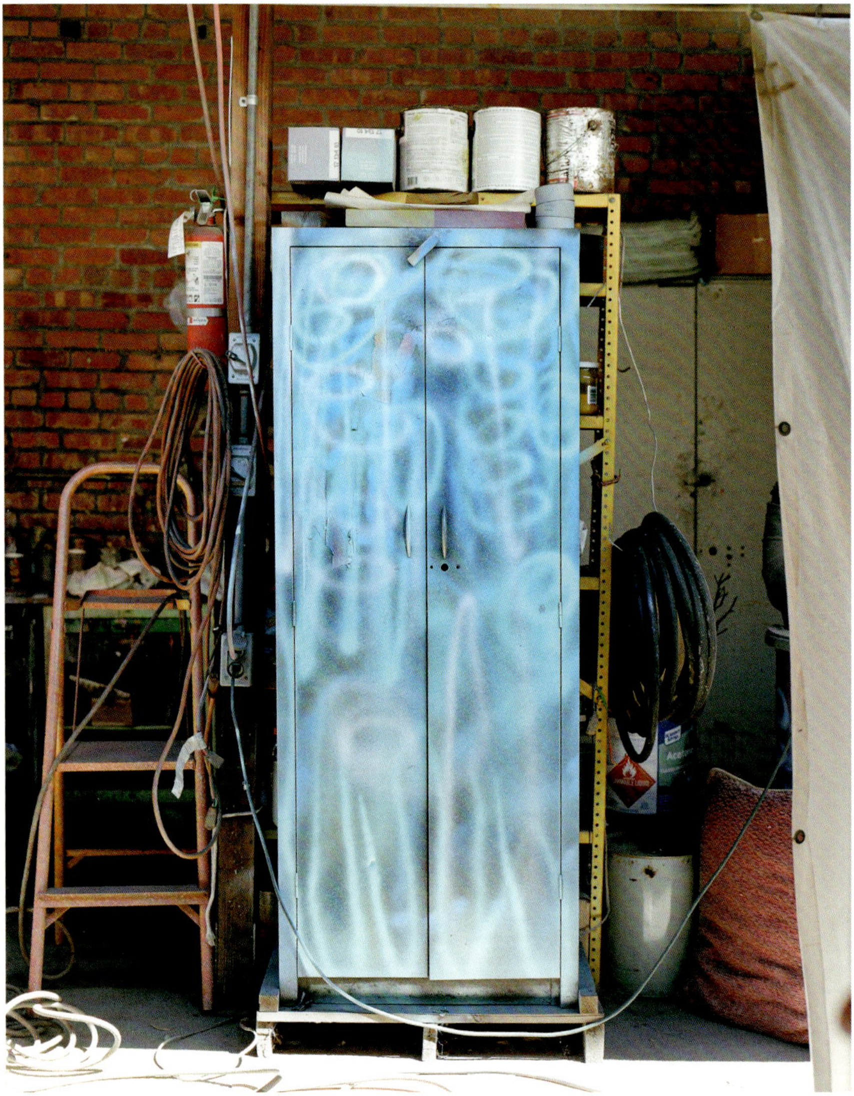

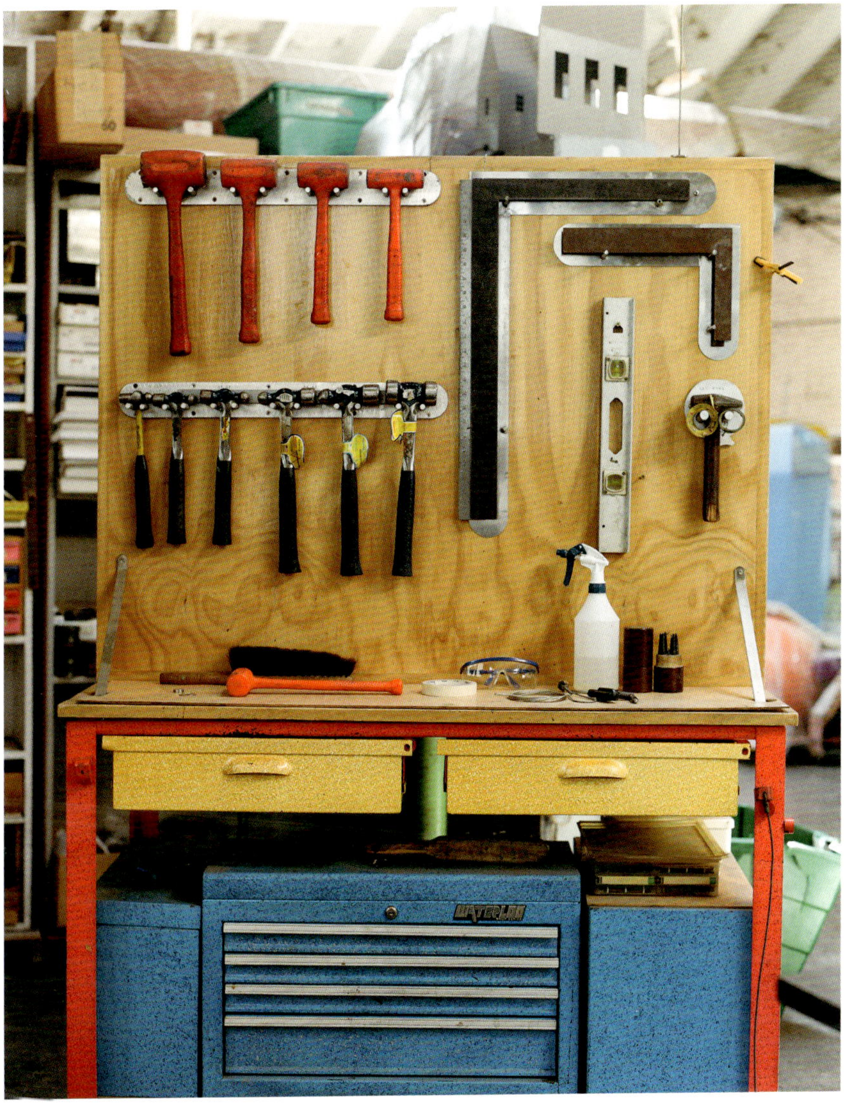

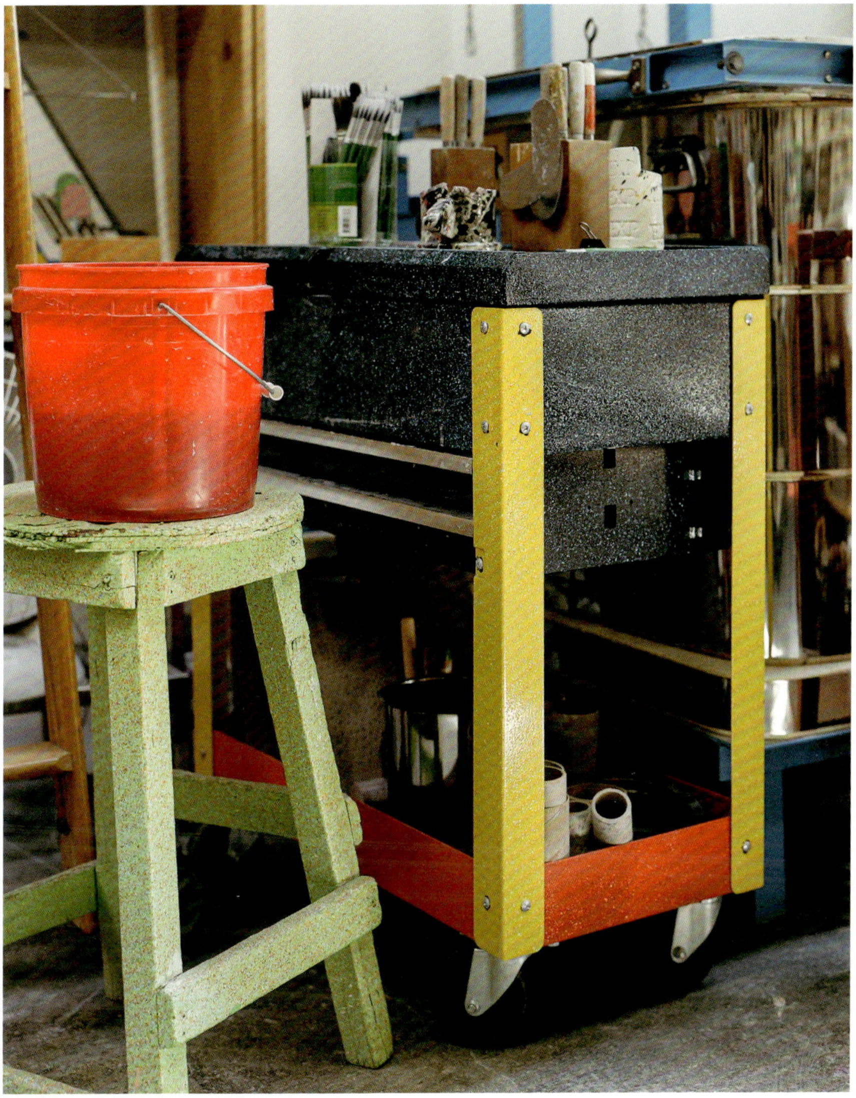

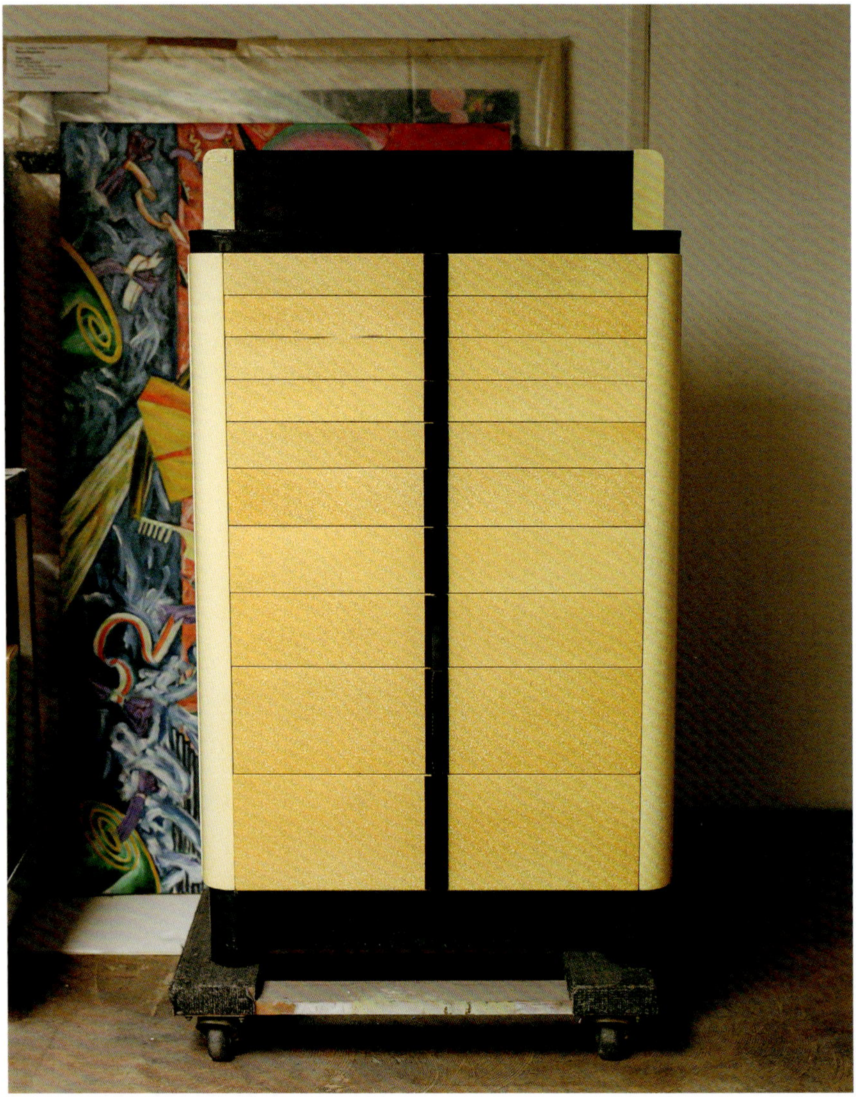

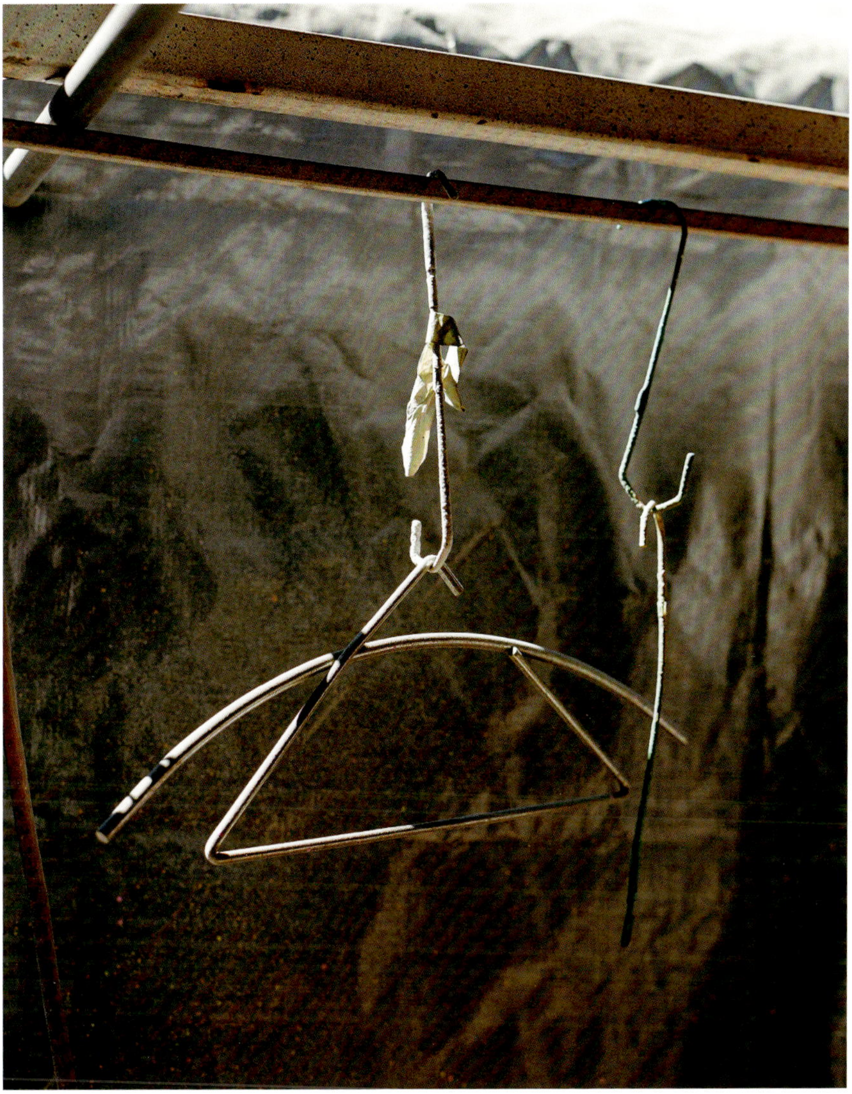

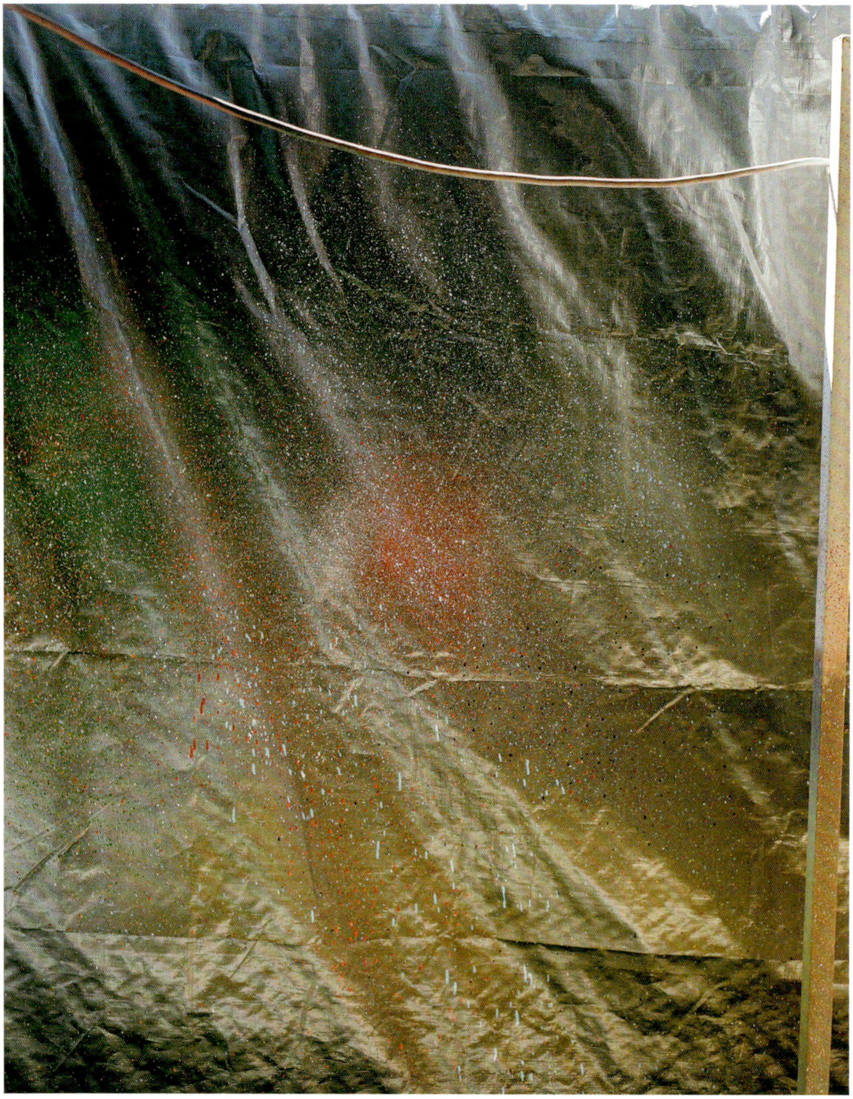

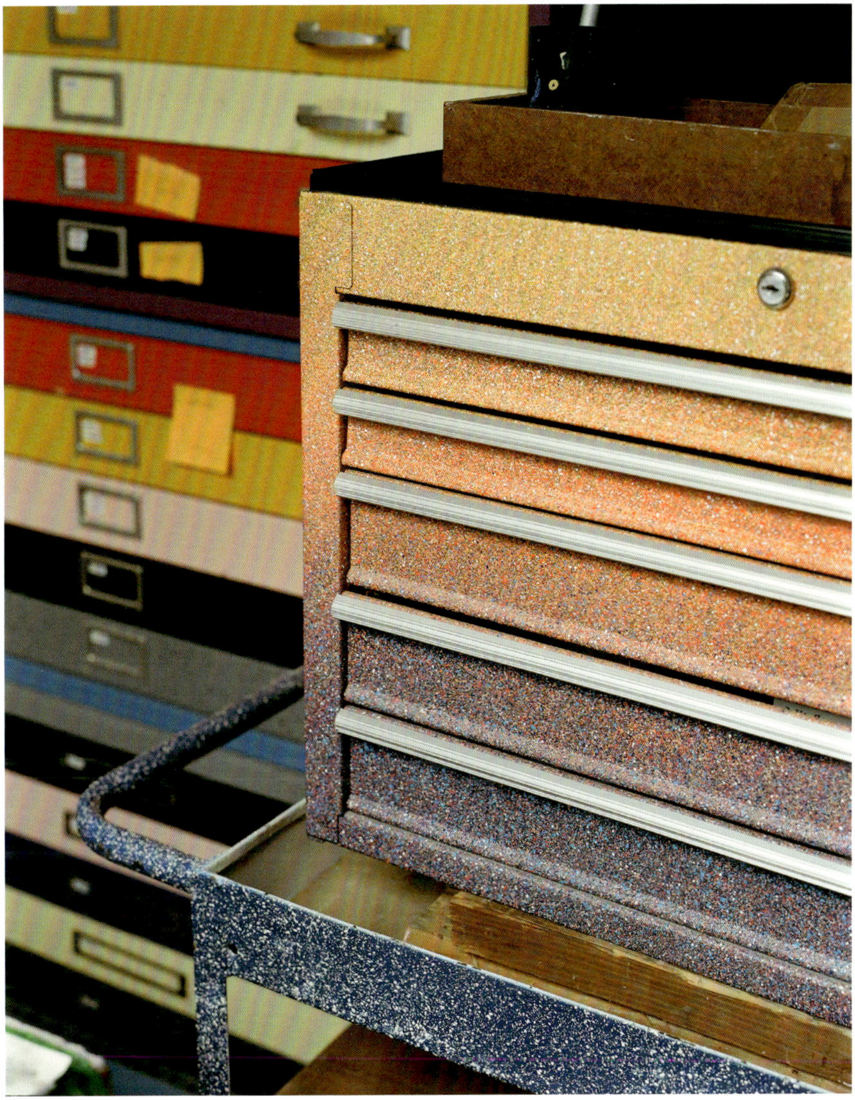

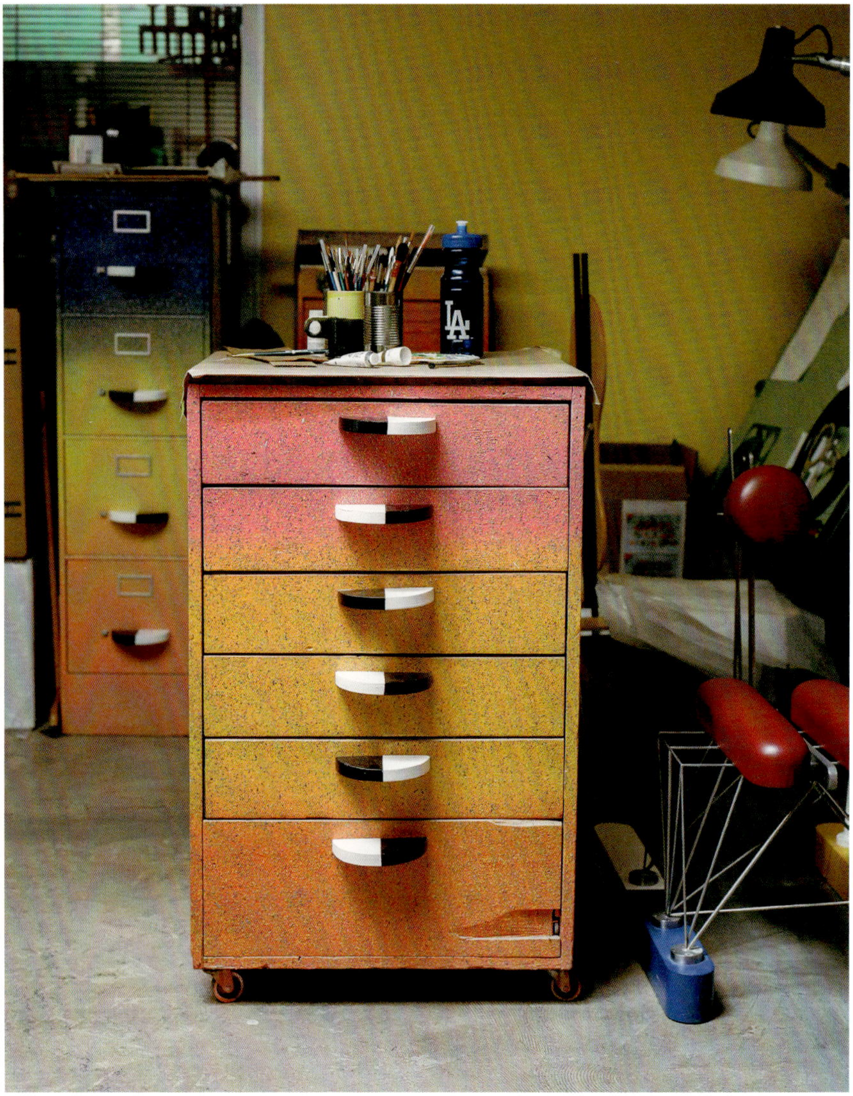
LA

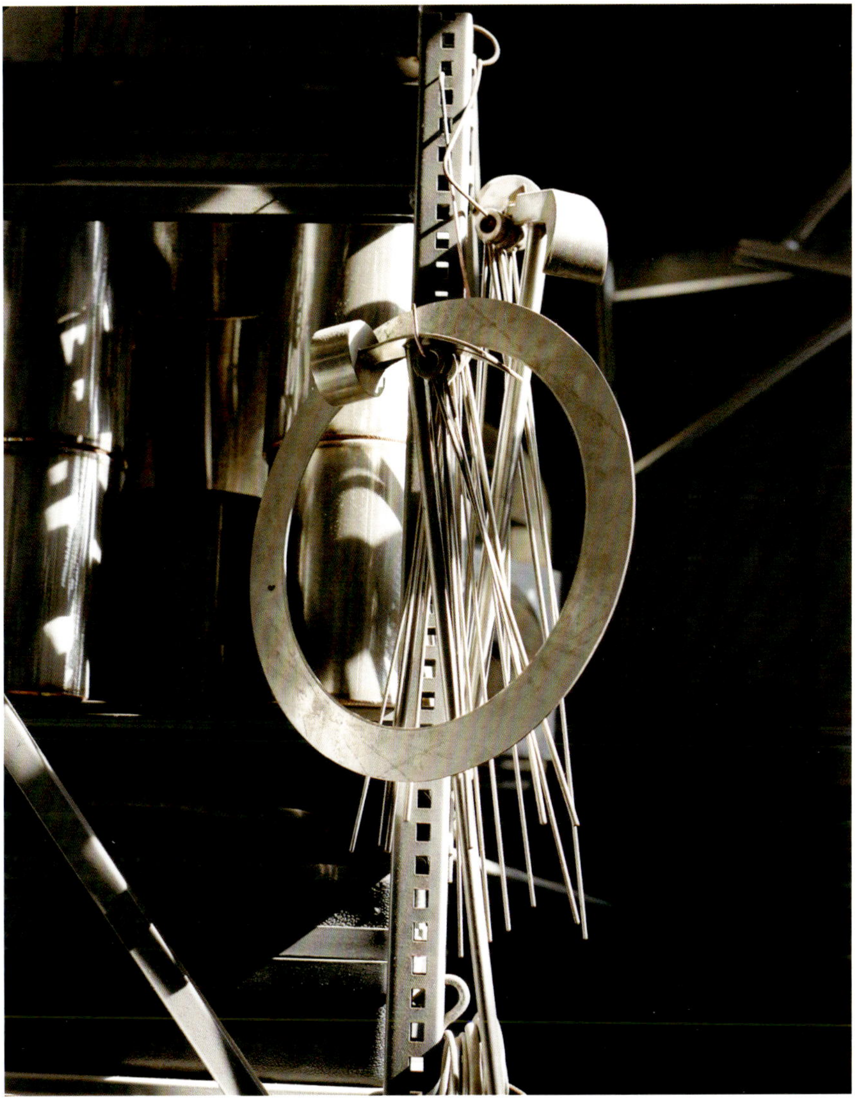

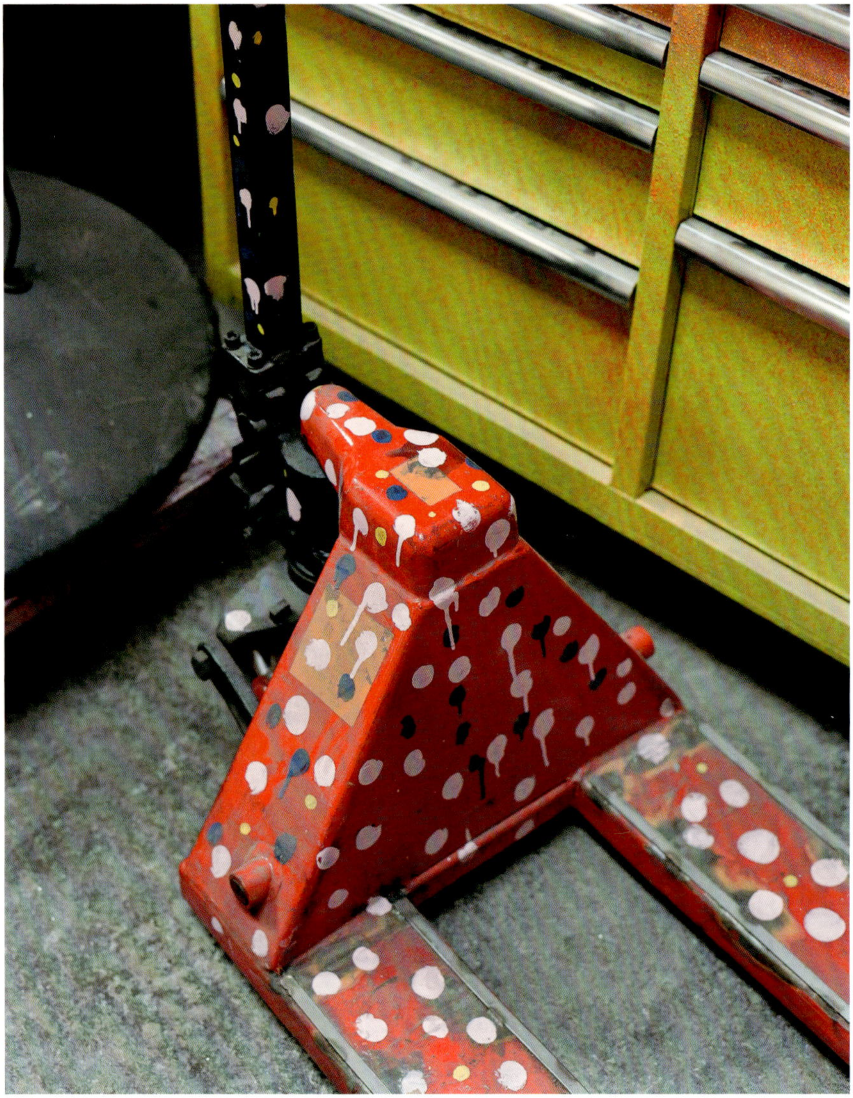

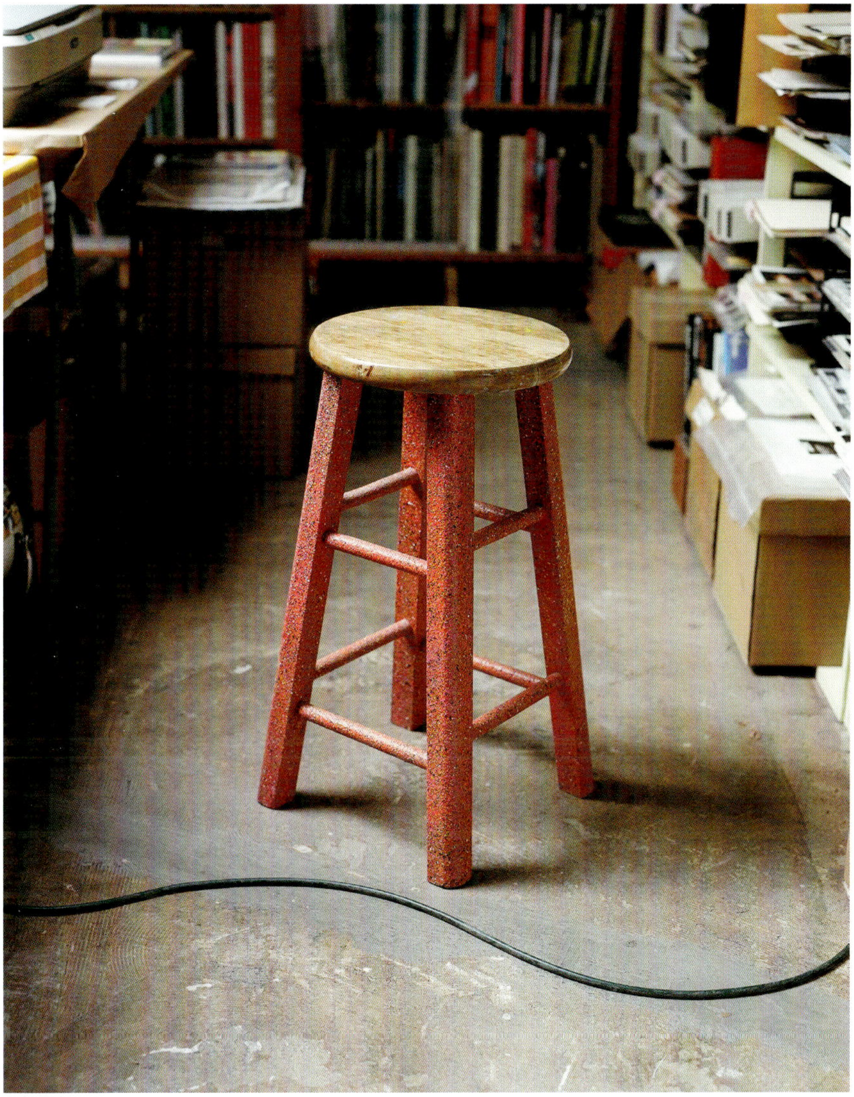

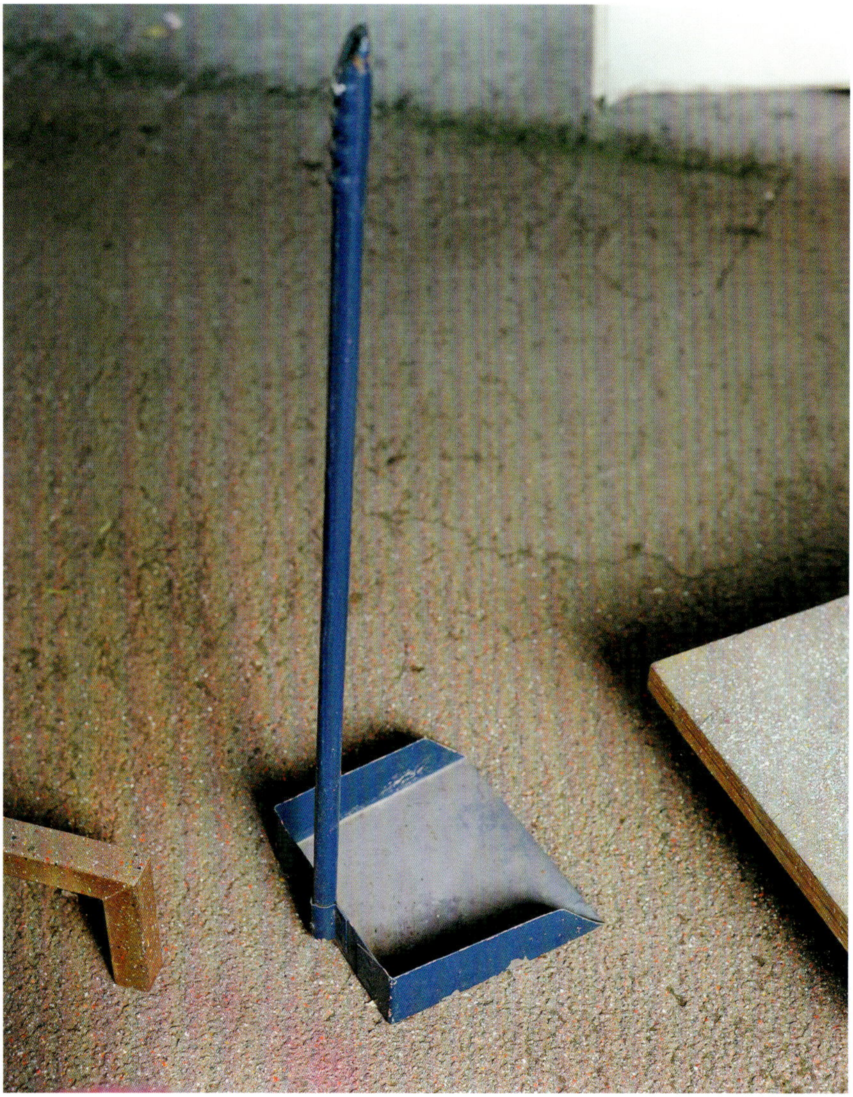

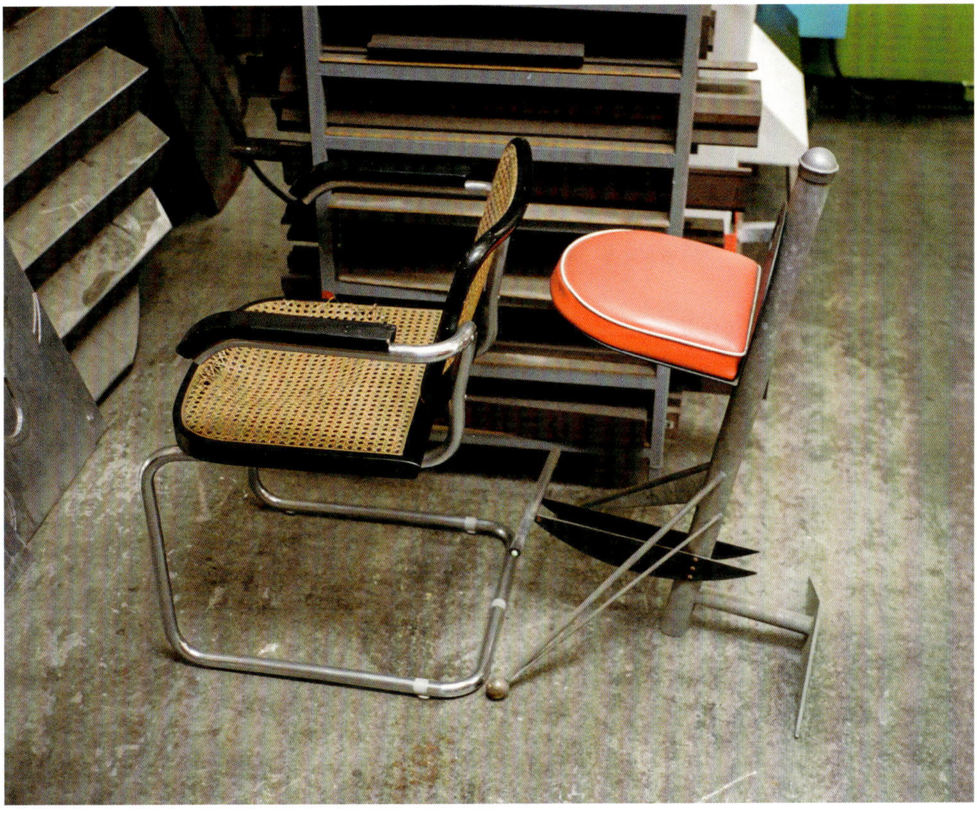

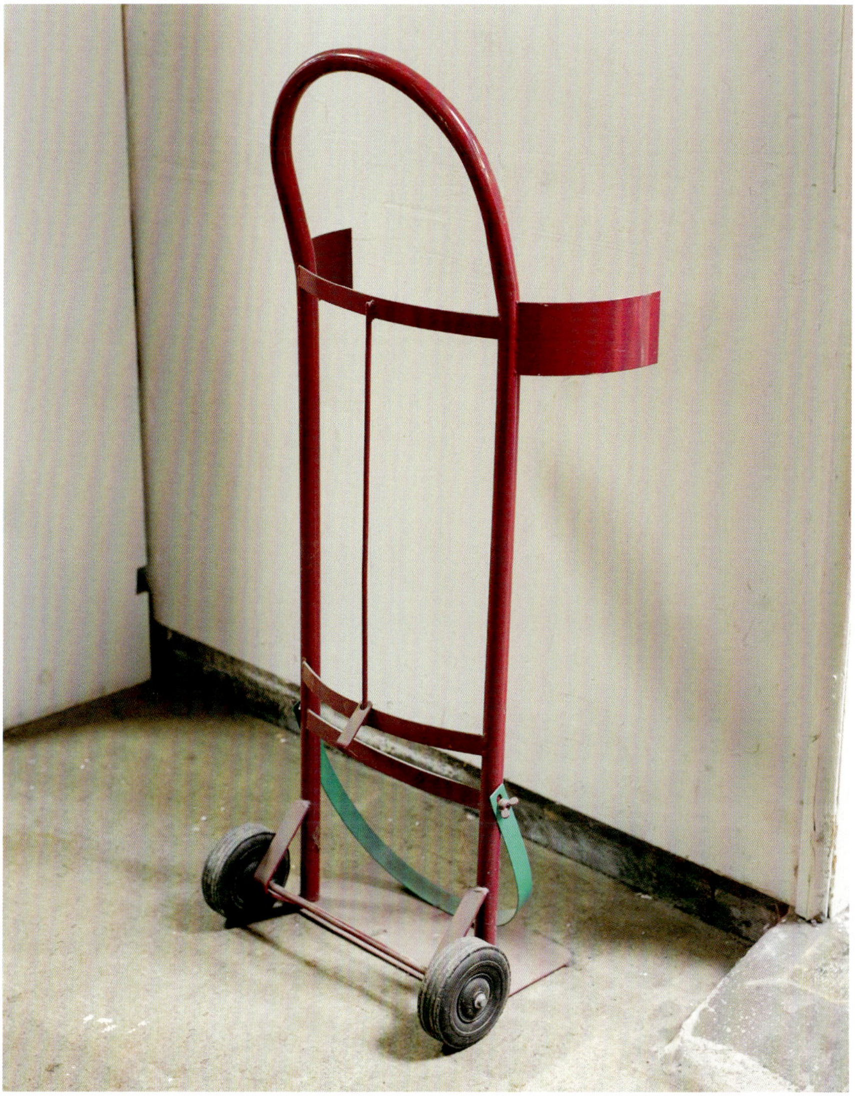

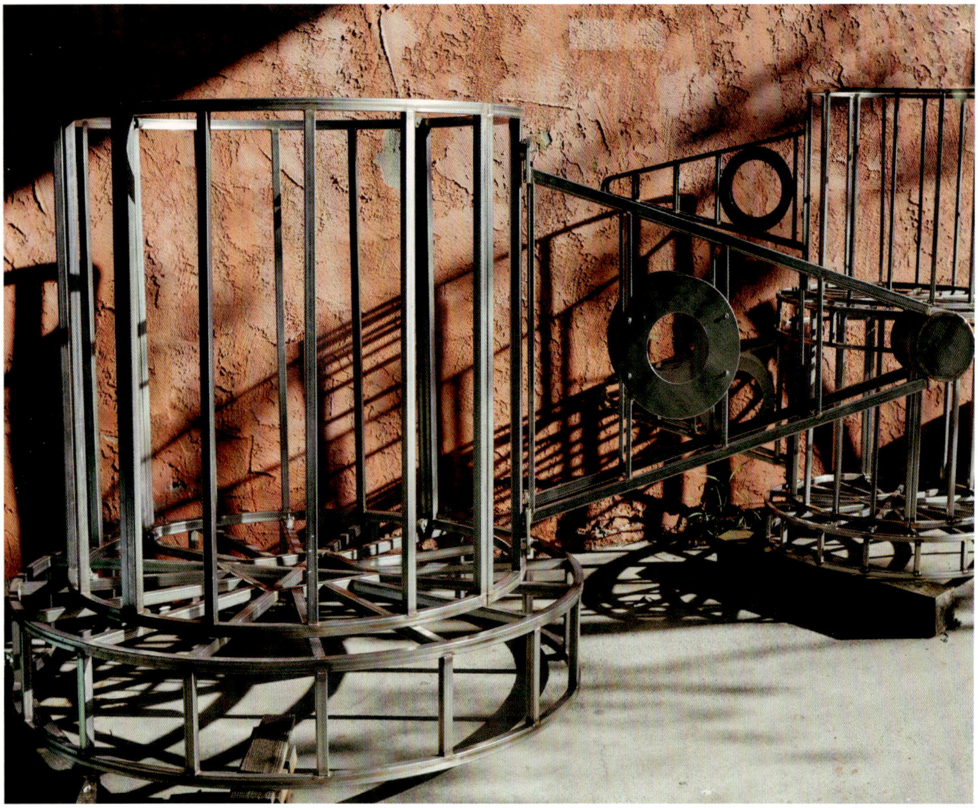

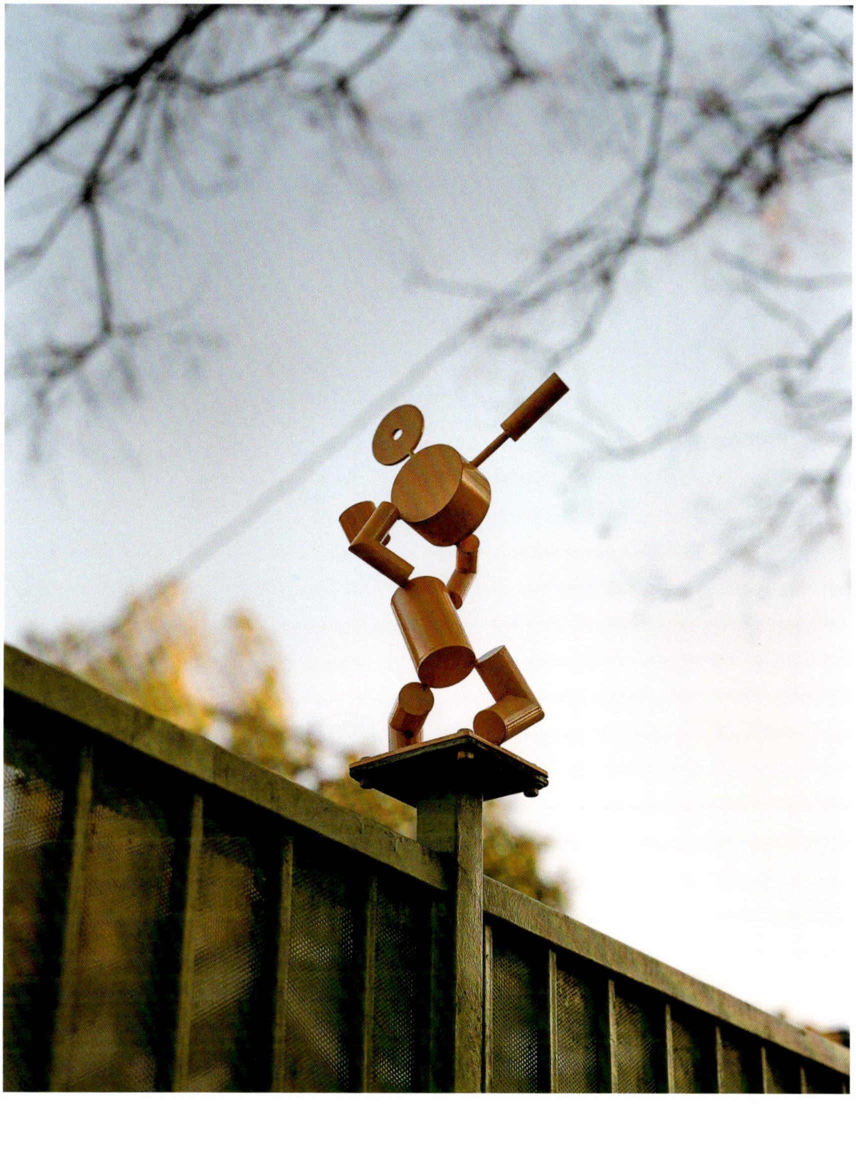

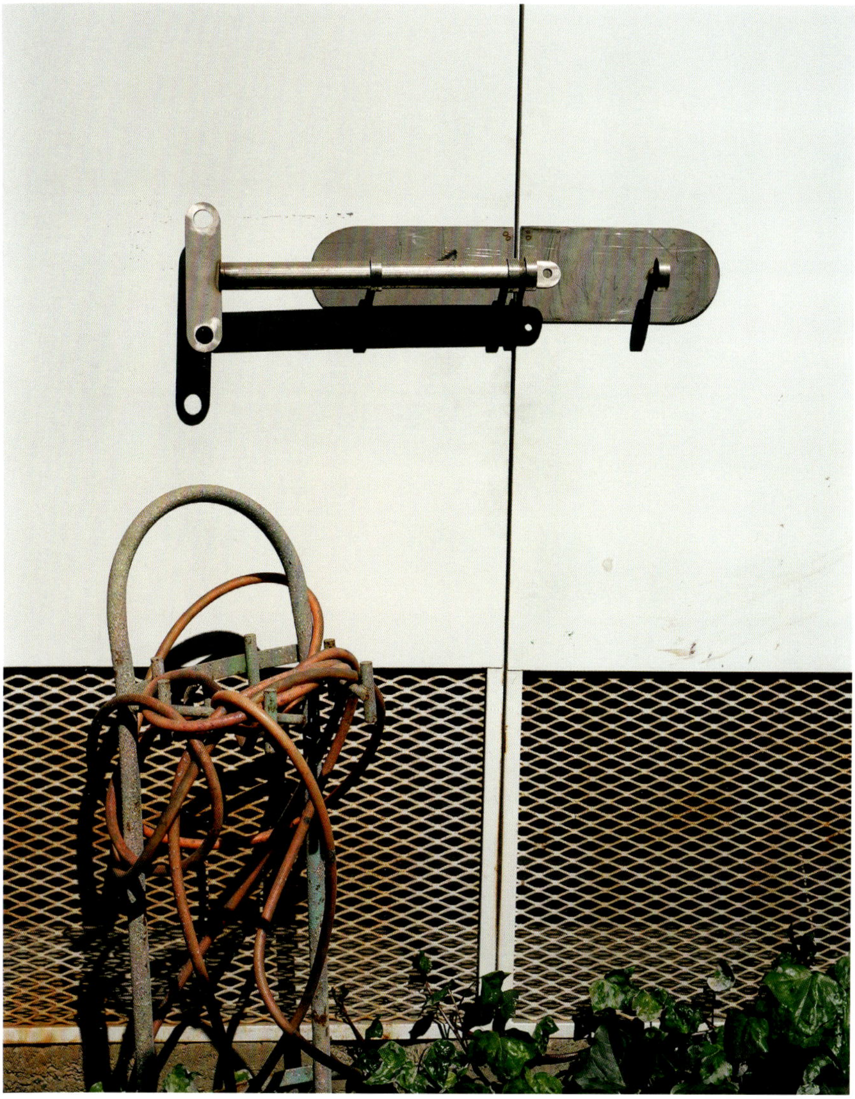

Studio / Peter Shire

Photographs by Brian W. Ferry

Published by
Pre–Echo Press

PE-14

Edition of 1,000 copies

Design by Joseph Logan and Katy Nelson of Joseph Logan Design

Special thanks
Peter Shire, Lisa Tchakmakian, the studio, and the team at EXP Pottery, Claire Cottrell,
Bleeker Digital Solutions NYC, and Photo Impact Imaging Los Angeles

ISBN: 978-1-63821-858-6